PHILIP PULLMAN

Philip Pullman was born in Norwich and educated in England, Zimbabwe, Australia and Wales. He studied English at Exeter College, Oxford. His first children's book, *Count Karlstein*, was published in 1982. To date, he has published thirty-three books, read by children and adults alike. His most famous work is *His Dark Materials*. These books have been honoured by several prizes, including the Carnegie Medal, the Guardian Children's Book Prize, and (for *The Amber Spyglass*) the Whitbread Book of the Year Award – the first time that prize had been given to a children's book. Pullman has received numerous other awards, including the Eleanor Farjeon Award and the Astrid Lindgren Award. He was knighted in the 2019 New Year's Honours list for services to literature.

Selected works by Philip Pullman

THE BOOK OF DUST
La Belle Sauvage
The Secret Commonwealth

HIS DARK MATERIALS
Northern Lights
The Subtle Knife
The Amber Spyglass

SHORT STORIES FROM THE WORLD OF HIS DARK MATERIALS AND THE BOOK OF DUST
Lyra's Oxford
Once Upon a Time in the North
Serpentine
The Collectors

NON-FICTION
Dæmon Voices: Essays on Storytelling

BRYONY LAVERY

Bryony Lavery's play *Frozen* won the TMA Best Play Award, the Eileen Anderson Central Television Award, and was produced at Birmingham Rep, the National Theatre, and then on Broadway where it was nominated for four Tony Awards; it was revived in the West End at the Theatre Royal Haymarket. *Stockholm,* for Frantic Assembly, won the Wolff-Whiting Award for Best Play of 2008. *Beautiful Burnout for* the National Theatre of Scotland/Frantic Assembly received a Fringe First at Edinbugh.

Other theatre writing credits include *Oliver Twist* (Leeds Playhouse/Ramps on the Moon); The *Lovely Bones* (Liverpool Everyman & Playhouse, Birmingham Rep, Northern Stage and Royal and Derngate Northampton); *The Midnight Gang* (Chichester Festival Theatre); *The Borrowers* (Storyhouse and Grosvenor Park Open Air Theatre); *Brighton Rock* (Pilot Theatre); *Balls* (Stages Theatre Houston/59E59 Theatre NYC)

She is a fellow of the Royal Society of Literature, an honorary doctorate of Arts at De Montfort University and an Associate Artist at Birmingham Repertory Theatre.

Philip Pullman

THE BOOK OF DUST

La Belle Sauvage

adapted for the stage by
Bryony Lavery

NICK HERN BOOKS
London
www.nickhernbooks.co.uk

A Nick Hern Book

This adaptation of *The Book of Dust – La Belle Sauvage* first published in Great Britain as a paperback original in 2021 by Nick Hern Books Limited, The Glasshouse, 49a Goldhawk Road, London W12 8QP

The Book of Dust – La Belle Sauvage copyright (play) © 2021 Bryony Lavery
The Book of Dust – La Belle Sauvage copyright (book) © 2017 Philip Pullman

Philip Pullman and Bryony Lavery have asserted their right to be identified as the authors of this work

Cover design: Muse Creative Communications

Designed and typeset by Nick Hern Books, London
Printed in Great Britain by Mimeo Ltd, Huntingdon, Cambridgeshire PE29 6XX

A CIP catalogue record for this book is available from the British Library

ISBN 978 1 83904 030 6

Woodland CARBON
www.woodlandcarbon.co.uk
NICK HERN BOOKS
Printed on Carbon Captured paper

The Book of Dust – La Belle Sauvage was first performed at the Bridge Theatre, London, on 7 December 2021 (previews from 30 November). The cast was as follows:

HYENA/STELMARIA (ASRIEL'S DÆMON)/SISTER PAULINA	Julie Atherton
MRS POLSTEAD/SISTER MARIA THERESE/WITCH	Holly Atkins
MOTHER SUPERIOR/ PROFESSOR CLUNY	Wendy Mae Brown
GERARD BONNEVILLE	Pip Carter
MALCOLM POLSTEAD	Samuel Creasey
ALICE PARSLOW	Ella Dacres
MARISA COULTER	Ayesha Dharker
ASTA (MALCOLM'S DÆMON)	Heather Forster
DR HANNAH RELF	Naomi Frederick
CCD MAN/DRUNK/GOLDEN MONKEY	Richard James-Neale
LORD ASRIEL/GEORGE BOATWRIGHT	John Light
SISTER FENELLA/DORIS WHICHER	Dearbhla Molloy
ERIC/CCD MAN/PROFESSOR PAPADIMITRIOU	Tomi Ogbaro
ROBERT LUCKHURST/JESPER (HANNAH RELF'S DÆMON)/ CHARLIE BOATWRIGHT	Sid Sagar
LORD NUGENT/ENVOY OF THE MAGISTERIUM/HEADMASTER	Nick Sampson
BEN (ALICE'S DÆMON)/ANDREW	Sky Yang
LYRA	Adiya/Khalil/ Paloma/Sarah and others

All other parts played by members of the company

6

Director	Nicholas Hytner
Co-Directors	Emily Burns
	James Cousins
Designer	Bob Crowley
Puppet Designer & Director	Barnaby Dixon
Video Designer	Luke Halls
Lighting Designer	Jon Clark
Sound Designer	Paul Arditti
Composer	Grant Olding
Movement Director	James Cousins
Fight Director	Kate Waters
Illusions Director	Filipe J. Carvalho
Casting Director	Robert Sterne
Puppetry Producer	Glenn Holberton
Associate Designer	Jaimie Todd
Associate Video Designer	Zakk Hein
Associate Lighting Designer	Lily Dyble
Fight Captain	Richard James-Neale
Costume Supervisors	Helen Johnson
	Anna Lewis
Props Supervisor	Lily Mollgaard
Production Manager	Kate West

For Nick, Emily and James,
Most Delightful Dæmons of Dramaturgy

Characters

GODSTOW, OXFORD, ULVERCOTE

MALCOLM POLSTEAD, *of The Trout Inn*
    ASTA, *his dæmon*

ALICE PARSLOW
    BEN, *her dæmon*

BRENDA POLSTEAD, *Malcolm's mum, landlady of
    The Trout Inn*
    BRIAN, *her dæmon, a badger*

ROSEMARY, *scholar*

MURIEL, *scholar*

GEORGE BOATWRIGHT
    SALLY, *his dæmon, a staffie*

LORD NUGENT, *Lord Chancellor*
    LEMUR, *his dæmon*

ROBERT LUCKHURST, *fellow of Magdalen College*
    CAT, *Luckhurst's dæmon*

BENEDICTA, *Mother Superior of St Rosamund's Priory,
    Godstow*

SISTER FENELLA
SISTER KATHERINE
SISTER CLARE
SISTER ISOBEL   }   *of the Order of St Rosamund*
SISTER ANNE
SISTER HELENA

LYRA, *a baby*
    PANTALAIMON, *her dæmon*

HEADMASTER *of Ulvercote Elementary School*

MRS SAVERY
MISS DAVIS   }   *teachers*
MISS DUKES

ANDREW WHICHER
ERIC
ROBBIE   }   *students at Ulvercote Elementary
FLORA   School*
RUBY

DR HANNAH RELF, *fellow of St Sophia's College*
    JESPER, *her dæmon*
GERARD BONNEVILLE
    HYENA, *his dæmon*
PAPADIMITRIOU
ADNAN   } *members of the opposition at*
YASMIN AL KHASY   *Oakley Street*
CLUNY

LONDON
MARISA COULTER
    GOLDEN MONKEY, *her dæmon*
LORD ASRIEL
    SNOW LEOPARD, *his dæmon*
MICHAEL WHARTON *of the Magisterium*

THE FLOOD
CHARLIE, *George Boatwright's partner*
DORIS WHICHER, *Andrew's aunt*
CHILD PROTECTION OFFICER
TILDA VASSARA, *a witch*
SISTER MARIA THERESE   } *Sisters of Holy Obedience*
SISTER PAULINA

Plus
CUSTOMERS AT THE TROUT INN
CCD MEN
NUNS
STUDENTS
SERVANTS
GOVERNMENT OFFICIALS
REFUGEES
ARMED POLICEMEN
...and, of course, their DÆMONS

A forward slash / indicates overlapping speech.

This text went to press before the end of rehearsals and so may differ slightly from the play as performed.

ACT ONE

1. The Trout Inn

MALCOLM. I'm Malcolm Polstead.
  I was twelve when all this began, still living with my mum at
  The Trout Inn, Godstow.

MRS POLSTEAD (*bustling*). Look sharp, / Malcolm.

MALCOLM. Large Terrace with stunning views of The Thames.
  Traditional Home-cooked Food.
  We serve *eighteen* Traditional-brewed / Ales...

MRS POLSTEAD. Opening time... *one* minute, Malcolm!

MALCOLM. And of course...
  my dæmon...
  Asta...
  Hadn't *settled* yet, had you?

  ASTA *appears from somewhere about* MALCOLM*'s
  person... a mouse.*

ASTA. Well... *you* hadn't settled. You were only twelve.

MALCOLM. I know.

ASTA. *Mouse* one minute, *lizard* the next...

MALCOLM. The day this began... At this moment a...
  kingfisher.
  You were very changeable.

ASTA. Only because *you* were. It was *puberty.*

MALCOLM. I *know.*

ASTA. Honestly, I was glad when that was over. So I could be
  just *one* thing.

MRS POLSTEAD. Malcolm! *Working* not *thinking*!

MALCOLM. Mum, when did your Brian settle as a badger?

MRS POLSTEAD. Was it sixteen, Brian?

BRIAN. Seventeen. When you came to work here.

MALCOLM. Why did you finally settle as a *badger*, Brian?

BRIAN. She's a pub landlady. We needed a strong body.

MRS POLSTEAD. And big paws! *Customers*, Malcolm!

TROUT CUSTOMERS *and their* DÆMONS *arrive*.

MALCOLM. All our regular customers were great *arguers*…
for instance they'd argue about our terrible weather.

TROUT CUSTOMERS. Stopped raining at last.
No it's still spitting.
I remember when summer / allus meant *sun*.
It's something messing with the sky…
No… It's something stirring up the water…

MALCOLM. The scholars from Oxford downriver were great
arguers.

ROSEMARY. You're not *seriously* talking about the uncertainty
principle…???

MURIEL. You *must* admit there is *inherent* uncertainty
in the act of measuring a variable of a particle…

MALCOLM. What's the uncertainty principle, Professor?

MURIEL. Well, that's an interesting question, Malcolm.

ROSEMARY. No, it's really *not*!
(*Glasses are empty.*) Another?

MALCOLM *and* MRS POLSTEAD *get busy serving*.

GEORGE BOATWRIGHT. Brenda! Another pint of *Old
Traditional* when you're ready!

MRS POLSTEAD. That's your *third*, George Boatwright.

GEORGE BOATWRIGHT. I'm drinking to forget these *woeful*
election results, Brenda.

MALCOLM. There'd just been an election.

TROUT CUSTOMERS. What about this election / then?
    Well... I'm *very* pleased!
    Well, I'm / not!
    You can stop that *crowing*!
    I thought it couldn't / get worse!
    Well, it just did!
    We're in for a rough ride now!

MALCOLM. The scholars even argued about *their dæmons*!

ROSEMARY. We know the *settled form* of the dæmon reflects
    its person's *character* /

    All DÆMONS *take an interest in this.*

MURIEL. / Well that's the current thinking,
    but *I* would argue it is an external manifestation of the *soul*.

ROSEMARY. But we agree the dæmon chooses its settled
    form, ergo
    humans who don't like their settled form are *conflicted*...

MURIEL. Until they achieve self-acceptance.

MALCOLM. Mum's dæmon Brian just dozes all the time
    while Mum *bustles*.
    Mum, are *you* conflicted?

MRS POLSTEAD. No, Malcolm, I'm just run off my feet being
    civil to everybody!

BRIAN. So I helps out by having her *true* opinions and keeping
    them to ourselves.
    Right, Brenda?

MRS POLSTEAD. Right, Brian.

GEORGE BOATWRIGHT. Unfortunately, me and hers –
    (*His* STAFFIE DÆMON.) made the other way round.
    I got all the opinions... *she* keeps her mouth zipped.
    Put a half of Old Traditional in there, Brenda.

MRS POLSTEAD. That'll be *three and a half*, George
    Boatwright.

GEORGE BOATWRIGHT. It's my silent protest, Brenda!

MALCOLM. Then…
two strangers entered our pub,
and everybody's life changed.

LORD NUGENT *and* ROBERT LUCKHURST, *with their*
DÆMONS, *enter the pub. Umbrellas. They're soaking.*
Stand waiting.

TROUT CUSTOMERS. See who *that* is?
What?
There! By the / door!
Just come in!
Who! / Who?
Lord Nugent!
The Lord Chancellor / Lord Nugent?
The 'Lord Chancellor of Bloody England' / Lord Nugent?
Don't look! / *It is him!*
A bloody lemur!
That's his dæmon alright…
A bloody lemur!

NUGENT. I've been spotted.

MRS POLSTEAD. Lord Nugent!
The Trout Inn is *very honoured.*
Sir! Sirs! Do sit down.
Let me – (*She takes their umbrellas as…*)
My son Malcolm will take your orders.
Malcolm…!

MALCOLM *stands ready to take orders near* NUGENT
and LUCKHURST, *so he hears…*

LUCKHURST. This is bad this is bad you're too conspicuous.

NUGENT. We can't leave now… it would look odd… calm
down, Robert.
Nobody saw us visit the nuns.

MALCOLM (*to* ASTA). The nuns?

LUCKHURST. But is the Priory secure?

NUGENT. We can trust the nuns to keep our delivery safe.

LUCKHURST. This feels dangerous.

NUGENT. *Everywhere* feels dangerous now, Robert.

LUCKHURST. Because it *is*.

NUGENT. One drink.
 (*To* MALCOLM.) Brandy. Make it a double.

MALCOLM. What sort, sir?

NUGENT. Whatever you have.

LUCKHURST. Whiskey. Any single malt. Just a single.

MALCOLM. One double brandy. Whiskey. Single single malt.
 Anything else, sirs?

NUGENT. No thank you.

LUCKHURST. Did that boy hear what you just said?

NUGENT. Don't think so.

MALCOLM. I've got big ears, so I *had* heard.

NUGENT. He's... what... twelve years old?

MALCOLM. Twelve / yes, but...

NUGENT. Who's he going to tell?

MALCOLM. Not deaf and not stupid.
 Alice!

 And ALICE, *who loathes* MALCOLM, *appears*.

ALICE. Yes? *Professor.*

MALCOLM. The single malt.

ALICE (*to* BEN). Here we go, Ben.

BEN. Pushing us about again.

MALCOLM. And the brandy.

ALICE. Right away, Professor.

MALCOLM. The good brandy...

ALICE. Oh, these for you and your girlfriend, Professor?

MALCOLM *ignores her.*

Who's your girlfriend again, Malcolm?

MALCOLM*'s ears go red or something.*

Awwwww, Malcolm, ain't you got a girlfriend?
Course you ain't! Never been kissed ave you, Professor?
Who'd kiss / you, *you ugly frog*?

MALCOLM/ASTA. Right that's IT!

He implodes into a ball of revenge, attacks ALICE.
Fight – human against human, dæmon against dæmon,
BRIAN *a reluctant participant.*

ASTA. I'll *kill* you!

BEN. I'll kill *you*!

BRIAN. Let em kill each other!

MRS POLSTEAD. Not again!

BRIAN. Give us all a bit of peace!

MRS POLSTEAD. No / fighting, / you two!

She separates them. ASTA *and* BEN *continue snarling and spitting at each other.*

MALCOLM. She *bit* / me!

ALICE. Thass gonna be *a bruise*!

MRS POLSTEAD. Serves you right, Alice Parslow.
You tease him and tease him then e erupts.
And serves *you* right, Malcolm cos
you should know by now not to *rise* to her!
(*To* ALICE.) You. Inside. Pots!
(*To* MALCOLM.) You. Outside.
Go to the Priory, ask if they're alright for butter!

As MALCOLM *storms from the pub:*

You can take your boat!

2. Canoe

His canoe La Belle Sauvage *is moored on the river outside the pub.*

MALCOLM. This is my canoe...
  (*He is fathoms deep in love with his canoe.*)
  La Belle Sauvage.
  (*Gets the paddle which he uses to point out...*)
  She's an eight foot seven-and-a-half-inch two-person Albion oak-bark canoe,
  self-painted,
  she comes with welded paddle sup/ports...

ASTA. That's enough de/tail... get in.

MALCOLM. *Two* welded paddled supports port and starboard, and an extra skeg for directional stab/ility...

ASTA. Too much inform/ation... *paddle*!

MALCOLM . She's my own personal river vessel,
  what I typically use
  (*He paddles out into the flow of the river.*)
  to get from The Trout on *this bank*
  upstream to *the Priory* on *that* bank.
  You *can* go over the bridge on the Godstow Road...
  (*Points where.*)
  If you ent got boatage it's a bit quicker.
  But this afternoon for the first time in *days* it weren't raining,
  and I was in a canoe-ing mood.
  (*He canoes.*)
  The sisters were using this first *dry* spell for ages to do gardening.

  The SISTERS OF ST ROSAMUND *appear, neither calm nor serene,*
  carrying tools and dressed for bad-weather gardening,
  habits, wellingtons, rubber gloves.
  They push wheelbarrows filled with seed potatoes, and are led by BENEDICTA, *the Mother Superior.*

BENEDICTA. O gracious lord,
  in these troubled times,

with these new and perplexing challenges,
show us how we must serve you /...
O gracious lord help us.

MALCOLM. Let's ask them about Lord Nugent.

ASTA. Why the weird visit from the Lord Chancellor of
England?

MALCOLM. Also I'm *starving*...

ASTA. And it must be nearly their dinnertime!

3. The Priory

Outside the Priory.

BENEDICTA. Gardening, sisters. Anyone watching can see
we're just...
(*Looks anxiously out.*)

FENELLA (*blessing the tools*). Lord, make these ancient tools
last for one more planting season.
Make these potatoes we plant
feed every hungry nun this approaching wet winter.

MALCOLM. Reverend Mother! / Hello, everybody, hello!

BENEDICTA. Malcolm!... Oh dear... we didn't expect / you...

SISTERS FENELLA, CLARE, ISOBEL, ANNE,
KATHERINE, HELENA (*mendaciously and jittery*).
Malc/olm! Are you alone?
How very lovely to / see you!
Aren't you pleased the rain's / stopped?
As you see we are / all –
We're *gardening*!

MALCOLM. Can I help, it must be near your / dinnertime?

BENEDICTA. That would be very kind of you. Sister
Katherine, supply Malcolm with a tool.

FENELLA. Malcolm dear… we're trying *Maris Pipers* this time, because we were a bit disappointed in those *Anyas* you and I put in last year.

ANNE. We found them too *waxy* for mashed potatoes.

KATHERINE. And you know how we all like mashed potatoes, Malcolm!

MALCOLM. Me too! With stew! Are the chitted potatoes in the wheel/barrows?

FENELLA. Oh! Malcolm no… No! Reverend / Mother!

The NUNS *watch in suspended horror as in the wheelbarrow…*

MALCOLM. Oh, it's a baby!

KATHERINE. Hand under the head, Malcolm.

ANNE. And under the bottom.

MALCOLM (*he scopes her*). I've never seen one of these *close up*! (*He picks her up.*) Asta… look at his hands!

FENELLA. *Her* hands, Malcolm.

MALCOLM. They're *minuscule*.

ASTA. So are her baby feet!

BENEDICTA. This is unfortunate, Mal/colm…

MALCOLM. She's smiling! (*He focuses on her.*)
Hello… I'm *Malcolm*…

She focuses on him.

She's looking at me!

She is.

Hello, I'm Malcolm.
Who are *you*?

ASTA. Her dæmon is *minuscule*!
Hello, tiny chick!

PANTALAIMON *chirrups back.*

MALCOLM. He's trying to talk!
Who are you?

PANTALAIMON *tries to tell him, very chatty.*
Seeing MALCOLM *laughing makes* LYRA *laugh too.*

Oh look, she's laughing!

She gets the hiccups.

And now she's got hiccups…

Each time she hics, her dæmon PANTALAIMON *jumps… it is instant four-way love.*

BENEDICTA. Oh dear…

FENELLA. We're making too much *noise.*

They scan the dangerous world…
SISTERS *flock round* MALCOLM… CLARE *takes the baby off him.*

CLARE. Hand her to me, Malcolm.

MALCOLM. Everything about her is perfect, isn't it, Sister / Fenella?

FENELLA. Except she's woken / up!

KATHERINE. *Again?*

FENELLA. Oh, now she's cry/ing… [*Or 'She's going to cry.'*]

KATHERINE. She's hun/gry… I'd forgotten babies ate so often.

FENELLA. Sister Clare… take her and give her some milk!

SISTER CLARE *takes* LYRA *off.*

BENEDICTA. And keep watch.

FENELLA (*sniffs*). And change her. *I'd* forgotten babies – (*Mouthing.*) *pooed* so often…

MALCOLM. How do maiden ladies know how to look after babies?

FENELLA. You'd be surprised at what we know!
We do go out in the world, Malcolm.

MALCOLM. How come you're looking after this baby, Sister Fenella?

BENEDICTA. Malcolm. It is unfortunate that we let you see Lyra.

MALCOLM. Lyra?
That's the name of a constellation... on my star / map...

BENEDICTA. Malcolm, you're such a knowledg/eable boy.

MALCOLM. What's her dæmon called, he's / brilliant?

BENEDICTA. He's Pantalaimon.

MALCOLM. Wow that's a long name / for a little –

BENEDICTA. Malcolm, be quiet and listen.
Malcolm, you're our *dear* friend...
You do us so many kindnesses...

FENELLA. He's my trusted vegetable peeler when my arthritis is bad, / aren't you, Malcolm?

BENEDICTA. So, I think I must *trust* you to keep the knowledge of this baby *to yourself*!
Malcolm, promise on your *life* to tell no one.

MALCOLM. Okay.

BENEDICTA. I need your sacred promise.

MALCOLM. I promise.
(*Beat.*)
Why? Where did she come from?

BENEDICTA. I can't tell you that, Malcolm.

MALCOLM. Did Lord Nugent bring her?

FENELLA. O sweet holy Jesus.

MALCOLM. It *was*, wasn't it?
Is that what Lord Chancellors do? Look out for babies?

BENEDICTA. Why do you think Lord Nugent brought her?

MALCOLM. He was at the inn with another man.

    BENEDICTA *goes very still.*

I put two and two together…
Why did they give you Lyra? Hasn't she got any parents?

Beat. All the SISTERS *look to* BENEDICTA *for guidance.*

BENEDICTA. Not ones who *care* for her.
Gracious Father… may *this* be the right path…
Malcolm, the child was in the care of the court,
but Lord Nugent has removed her and entrusted her into
our care.

MALCOLM. Removed her from court?
Why?

BENEDICTA. *This* is what is making me very nervous because
I don't really know why.

FENELLA. It's very perplexing.

BENEDICTA. The Lord Chancellor has forbidden us to tell
anyone from the government.

KATHERINE. Or the Magisterium.

ISOBEL. Which is almost the same thing now.

FENELLA. Why can't a member of the government trust his
own government?
And why does Lord Nugent say that we must keep Lyra
a secret from our own Church?

BENEDICTA. He won't tell us.

FENELLA. He seems to think we cannot trust our own Church!

BENEDICTA. We inhabit a world of doubt.
It is therefore very perplexing to know quite who to trust!
So for the time being, Malcolm, we trust *no one.*
Not your mother, none of your friends.
Not one word. Do you understand?

MALCOLM. Yes.

BENEDICTA. *Promise!*

MALCOLM. *Promise!*

BENEDICTA. And now look at the sky!
   More rain, Holy Father?

   Dark clouds.

   We should get inside,
   Sister Katherine… go see if Sister Clare has fastened the
   nappy *securely* this time!
   Sister Fenella… *stew*!

MALCOLM. You're having stew…?

BENEDICTA. Malcolm…
   perhaps dinner another day?
   Perhaps… go birdwatching instead!
   Before it starts to rain again!

   MALCOLM *gets back in his canoe.* NUNS *exeunt.*

MALCOLM. Lyra… that's the name of a constellation,
   one of eighty-eight constellations listed by *P-tolemy*…

BENEDICTA (*disappearing, gently*). Tolemy.

MALCOLM (*correct pronunciation*). Ptolemy.

ASTA. *Canoe*, Malcolm…

MALCOLM (*into canoe as…*). On star maps it's represented by
   an *eagle* carrying a *lyre*…

ASTA. *Lecturing.*

MALCOLM. *Sorry.*
   (*Beat.*)
   Personality defect. Sorry…

   A sound of two great-crested grebes.

4. Bird Watching

On the river.

ASTA. Great-crested grebes!

MALCOLM. They're nesting same place as last year…
(*They watch the grebes*.)
Grebes are different from swans and ducks and geese,
in having lobed toes…

ASTA. Enough lobed toes, / Malcolm…

MALCOLM. When things get dangerous, they prefer to *dive*
rather than *fly*…

LUCKHURST (*beneath a tree*). Be careful. *Be careful!*

CAT. I will. *I will!*

LUCKHURST. *Here, take it.*

MALCOLM. That's Lord Nugent's friend from the pub! What's
he doing?

ASTA. His dæmon's climbing up that tree.

MALCOLM. Why?

ASTA. I'll go check.

ASTA *becomes a kingfisher again, hovers over*
LUCKHURST*'s* CAT DÆMON. *Two* CCD MEN *appear in*
the background, in dark coats, one with VIXEN DÆMON,
the other a LARGE BIRD. *They watch.*

CCD! CCD. They're watching him!

LUCKHURST. Here. Don't drop it, / don't drop it!

CAT (*opens her mouth to say*). I won't! (*Drops it.*)

LUCKHURST. You dropped it, you *idiot*!

CAT. *You* idiot!

MALCOLM. What did she drop?

ASTA. Like a nut. About the size of a nut.

MALCOLM. Did you see where it went?

ASTA. I think so.

LUCKHURST. Finditfindit!

CAT. Ican'tseeitwheredidit*go*?

MALCOLM. CCD are *very* interested.

ASTA. That's not good.

MALCOLM. He's seen them.

LUCKHURST. CCD! *Hurry up!*

CAT. I can't find it *I can't find it*!

LUCKHURST. They're coming over leave it LEAVE IT!
Evening.

>*Reluctantly he gives up the search,* CAT *on his shoulder.*
>*Both try to look calm and pass the* CCD MEN.
>LUCKHURST *nods to* CCD MEN. *They come either side of*
>*him and each takes one of his arms.*

ASTA. They've got him! Get down, get down.

MALCOLM. Sssh!

>*They are very still as* LUCKHURST *struggles, until he*
>*suddenly sags, like they've tasered him.* CCD *walk him off.*
>*The* CAT DÆMON *follows, dejected and mewing pitifully.*

ASTA. What will they do to him?

MALCOLM. Don't think about it… let's see what he dropped.

>MALCOLM *and* ASTA *fast as they can to the spot…*
>*searching…*

ASTA. This must be it.
An acorn.
But weirdly heavy.

MALCOLM. It's a wooden acorn.
This is *brilliant* carving.
I think it opens…
(*He examines it more closely.*)
Should just *pull*… (*But it doesn't.*)
must *unscrew*… (*But it doesn't.*)

>ASTA *changes from a kingfisher into a cat.*

Don't change, I'm trying to concentrate…

ASTA. It's *interesting*…
Try twisting it the other way…

MALCOLM. That'll just do it up *tighter*… (*But it doesn't*.)
Oh it *doesn't*… (*He opens the acorn*.)
I've never seen that before, that's *brilliant*! And look.

ASTA. What?

MALCOLM. There's a paper rolled up inside it. It's a message.
(*Reads*.) 'Urgent. Top priority.
Please enquire through the alethiometer
if there is any connection between the particle Rusakov has
discovered
and the phenomenon called *Dust*.
The other side are taking a significant interest.
Tread carefully.'
No signature.

ASTA. '*The other side*.'

MALCOLM. *CCD*.

ASTA. Bound to be.

MALCOLM. What's *Dust*?

ASTA. Well, it's not *dust*-dust, is it…

MALCOLM. No.

ASTA. *Weird*.

MALCOLM. *And* what's – (*Wrong pronunciation*.) *an
alethiometer*…

ASTA. We need to look it up.

School bell…

Or ask a teacher.

SCHOOL PUPILS *and* TEACHERS *enter in a rush of
playground energy*.

MALCOLM *pockets the acorn as*…

5. School

School Hall of Ulvercote Elementary School.

HEADMASTER (*arriving*). *Sit down, everybody!*

    MALCOLM *joins cross-legged pupils. They're supposed to
    be not talking so… sotto voce, lips barely moving, eyes front.*

MALCOLM. Robbie.

ROBBIE. Malcolm.

MALCOLM. Eric.

HEADMASTER. Stop talking.

ERIC. Malcolm.

MALCOLM. Andrew.

ANDREW. Eric. Robbie.

HEADMASTER. I said STOP TALKING!
    (*With reluctance – this has all been forced upon him.*)
    Today we have a visitor from the Magisterium.
    Who *doesn't* know what the Magisterium is?
    (*No hands go up.*)
    The Magisterium, which you older boys will know is based
    in…?

MALCOLM. Geneva, sir.

HEADMASTER. *Geneva…* well remembered, Polstead…
    We *all* know the Magisterium has authority to –
    (*Reads reluctantly and with attitude from a card…*)
    'spread the Word of God through *authentic* interpretation.'
    (*Beat.*)
    This is a change from today's timetable.

    TEACHERS *have attitude… but only body language…*

    We have here today one of the country's foremost
    experimental theologians, who wants to introduce us all to –
    (*Consults card.*)
    'The League of St Alexander',
    Mrs Coulter.

MRS COULTER, *around thirty, beautifully dressed, with her*
GOLDEN MONKEY DÆMON.

MRS COULTER. Thank you, Headmaster.
Boys and girls,
our Holy Church has many different parts within it which go
to make up the Magisterium
and they all work together for the good of the Church
which is the same as the good of every one of us.
If you, boys and girls,
sometimes find this confusing…
let me tell you about Alexander
a very brave boy who lived long ago
at a time when Holy Church was struggling against many
evil gods.
Unhappily… Alexander's parents worshipped an evil god.
Then, one day, in the marketplace, Alexander heard a man
talk about Jesus Christ…
how he rose from the dead
and how anyone who believes in him will have everlasting
life…
and he went to his parents and said
'Dad. Mum. I want to be a Christian.'
But his parents wouldn't listen to him. They continued to
worship their evil god.
They even sheltered, in their house, people who believed in
that same evil god.
So in the middle of the night
soldiers went to that house to arrest them.
How did the soldiers know which house?
Alexander took a lamp up on to the flat roof
so they could see its light in all the darkness
and seize those evil people.
Next day
in the marketplace –
His parents and their friends were put to death.
Sad though he was, that brave boy continued to hunt down
people who didn't believe in Holy Church
and after his death
Alexander became a saint.
It is in memory of that bravest of boys

that I have set up the League of St Alexander
I wear this badge –
(*She shows a badge.*)
its emblem
is a picture of the lamp he carried to the roof
to signal where evil lives...
You think those days were long ago.
Today...
we all believe in the true God
we all cherish and love the Church.
This is a Christian country.
But there are new enemies of the Church
that say openly 'there is no God.'
Some of these enemies make speeches
write books
become famous...
we *know* who *they* are.
More worrying are the people we *don't* know about...
the people you see every day
your neighbours
your parents
your teachers...
have you heard anyone *you know* denying the truth
about God?
Mocking the Church?
Criticising it?
Telling lies about us?
The spirit of St Alexander lives on today
in every boy or girl who is brave enough to do what he did...
if you join the League you get this badge to wear
to continue Alexander's brave work
Who would like to join?

MALCOLM. You gonna join, Andrew?

ANDREW. Why would *I* join, Malcolm? I'm a saint already!

MALCOLM. How come?

ANDREW. St *Andrew* right?

MALCOLM. Is there a *St Malcolm*?

ANDREW. No! *You'll* have to join 'the League of St Andrew', Malcolm!
(*Friendly punch and exits*.)

MALCOLM. You wish!

ASTA. It's a very handsome badge…

MALCOLM. It's *snitching* though… isn't it? Dobbing in *your mum*?

ASTA. I *suppose*…
Anybody else we know doing something that we don't like? Get us a badge?

MALCOLM. Alice!

They like this.

ASTA. Let's try catch her saying something wrong!

They like this.
Beat.

MALCOLM. The *sisters* are behaving out of character, making us keep secrets.

ASTA. And they're doing secret stuff against the government.

MALCOLM. Is the government the same thing as the Magisterium? And is the CCD the same thing as the police?

ASTA. I think the police are the police and the CCD are *worse*.

MALCOLM. Let's ask Mum. See what *she* thinks.

6. A CCD Visit

The pub coalesces around them, ALICE *serving,*
MRS POLSTEAD *on a break,* GEORGE BOATWRIGHT
drinking to forget.
Watching vigilantly is DR HANNAH RELF.

MALCOLM. Mum...

MRS POLSTEAD. Not *now*, Malcolm, I'm on my break... go
on, George.

GEORGE BOATWRIGHT. If you mess with *the weather... it's*
gonna mess with *you*.
If you mess with the *water table... it's* gonna mess / with *you*.

MALCOLM. *Mum...*

MRS POLSTEAD. The rain never stops.
That river is just rising and rising and rising and...
Remember when we were kids, George?
Botley – everybody up to their ankles in water!
Osney – everybody up to their ankles in water!
St / Ebbe's...

GEORGE BOATWRIGHT. Are they doing anything about
flood risk?

MRS POLSTEAD. Are they *buffalo*!

MALCOLM. *Mum...*

ALICE. It's *things* in the water getting stirred up.

MRS POLSTEAD. Nonsense, Alice.

GEORGE BOATWRIGHT. Girl's not wrong, Brenda... you
don't want to get that river angry.

CCD MEN appear on the perimeter of the pub.

Don't look. Trouble's arrived.

The atmosphere changes to fear and stillmess. CCD MEN
have everyone's attention but no one looks directly at them.
They are nice as pie, their DÆMONS *are utterly chilling.*

CCD MAN 1. *Sorry* to interrupt... is the landlord / around?

MRS POLSTEAD. Land*lady*. That's me.

CCD MAN 1. Mrs… (*Proffers hand*.)

MRS POLSTEAD (*takes it*). Polstead. Brenda Polstead.

CCD MAN 1. Mrs Polstead.

ASTA. CCD!

MALCOLM. Can I help, Mum?

CCD MAN 1. Who's this?

MRS POLSTEAD. This is my son but he's only twelve.

CCD MAN 1 (*proffers hand*). Hello…

MALCOLM. Malcolm.

CCD MAN 1. You look like a clever boy, Malcolm. Do you know who Lord Nugent is?

MALCOLM. Yes, *sir*, he's / the…

MRS POLSTEAD. The Lord Chancellor of Eng/land…

CCD MAN 2. The *former* Lord Chancellor of Eng/land.

MRS POLSTEAD. Former. Sorry, sir.

CCD MAN 2. He lost his job this morning. Let Malcolm here answer.

CCD MAN 1. Was he ever here in this pub, Malcolm?

GEORGE BOATWRIGHT. We *all* saw him in here. What do you want to know?

GEORGE*'s boldness is at odds with his* DÆMON STAFFIE, *who is trembling*.

CCD MAN 1. I'm asking Malcolm. Was he alone?

MALCOLM. He was with a man who looked like he lived in a college / or something.

CCD MAN 1. Well remembered, Malcolm! What did they talk about?

Beat.

MALCOLM. They just ordered drinks, sir.

CCD MAN 2. *Just ordered drinks?*
  No chit-chat? That seems unlikely.

MALCOLM. Sorry, sir.

CCD MAN 1. What else? Malcolm?

MALCOLM. No, sir.

CCD MAN 2. School teaches you to tell the truth, right, lad?

MALCOLM. Yes, sir.

CCD MAN 1. Sit down. What else?

ASTA. *Tell* him.

CCD MAN 1. What else?

ASTA. *Tell* him.

MALCOLM. Nothing else – (*Beat*.) sir.

CCD MAN 1. Because that man's ended up drowned in the
  river, Malcolm.

CCD MAN 2. Robert Luckhurst. Doctor of Philosophy.

CCD MAN 1. Whatever *that* means.

CCD MAN 2. Means he's *supposed* to be clever.

CCD MAN 1. Not so clever now, is he?

MALCOLM. Did he just fall in?

CCD MAN 1. He must have.

CCD MAN 2. You seem upset. Not lying to me, are you,
  Malcolm?

MALCOLM. No, sir.

CCD MAN 2. Because we're very good at dealing with people
  who lie, / Malcolm…

GEORGE BOATWRIGHT (*big and bold,* STAFFIE DÆMON
  ditto). Alright. You've had your fun.
  You've bullied the boy enough.

CCD MAN 1. I beg your pardon?

GEORGE BOATWRIGHT. Yeah, go on… *beg my pardon*! And beg the lad's pardon, and beg *this country's* pardon for every bloody act of intimidation and browbeating and sheer bloody interfering in our lives… our decent honest lives you *Bully Boys* think / you can interfere with –

MRS POLSTEAD. George…

GEORGE BOATWRIGHT. I'm sorry, Brenda, but I'm up to *here* with this. This is our pub not yours, this is *our* leisure time not your *interrogation* time, this is *our* country not yours or your bloody Magister/ium!

MRS POLSTEAD. Leave it, / George…

CCD MAN 1. Malcolm, what's this man's name?

Waits. MALCOLM *doesn't answer, looks towards his mother, to* GEORGE BOATWRIGHT.

George… right? George *what*, Malcolm?

GEORGE BOATWRIGHT. My name's George *Boatwright, you bullying, bleeding* / *bastard.*

MRS POLSTEAD. George… your Charlie'll be wondering where you got to! You better leave now. Go on, come back when you're sober.

CCD MAN 1. George Boatwright. Come with us. Outside. Now. Seeing as you've got so much to say.

Nasty skirmish. CCD MEN *watch as their* DÆMONS *bully the* STAFFIE… *but* GEORGE BOATWRIGHT *escapes.* CCD MEN *pursue him.*

You're making it worse for yourself, George Boatman!

MRS POLSTEAD. Malcolm! Alright?

MALCOLM. Yes, Mum. You alright?

MRS POLSTEAD. If *you're* alright, I'm alright.

They have an embarrassed hug.

Don't worry about George. E's got more lives than a cat. Lady. There. Empty glass.

MALCOLM (*going over to her*). Can I take your order, miss?

HANNAH. That was a bit terrifying, wasn't it?

MALCOLM. Yes, miss.

HANNAH. There's a Cathay curse… 'May you live in
    interesting times.'
    Do you know it?

MALCOLM. No, miss. Can I take your order, miss?

HANNAH. Malcolm. It's Malcolm, isn't it?
    (*Private voice.*) Do you know anything about an acorn?

    MALCOLM *goes still*.

MALCOLM. An acorn off an oak tree, miss?

HANNAH. Not exactly.
    I see that you *do* know about an acorn *not* off a tree.
    A carved wooden acorn.
    (*Closes her book.*) I'm going to *forget* this book.
    (*Lays it on the table.*) You'll find it, return it to me.

    MALCOLM *picks it up*.

    My address is on the inside cover.

MALCOLM (*looks at the flyleaf*). 'St Sophia's.'

HANNAH. It's my college. In Oxford.
    Go to the porter's lodge. Ask for Dr Hannah Relf. That's me.
    Bring the acorn. As soon as you can.

    HANNAH *exits*.
    MALCOLM *passes* ALICE *returning from the kitchen
    carrying some full glasses of beer*.

ALICE. Get out of my way!

MALCOLM. *You* get out of *my* way!

    MALCOLM *exits as* ALICE *puts the full glasses down on
    a table*.

ALICE. Two glasses of Old Traditional from the new keg!

CUSTOMER 1 (*points to the table leg somewhere down
    between the two men*). Alice?

ALICE. What?

CUSTOMER 2. Table's wobbly.

ALICE. Oh, for crying out loud…

CUSTOMER 1. While you're down there.

> ALICE *gets out her cloth, bends down to wipe the table leg.*
> CUSTOMER 1 *puts his hand up her skirt.*

ALICE. Who done that?

CUSTOMER 1. Done what, Alice?

ALICE. Put their hand up my skirt.

CUSTOMER 2. Not me, Alice.

CUSTOMER 1. Nor me, Alice.

ALICE. That ever happens again…
 I won't even try to find who done it.
 I'll just break every finger on both your hands!

MRS POLSTEAD. What's going on?

ALICE. Someone made a mistake.
 Taking my break.
 (*Exits.*)

CUSTOMER 1. Thing is…
 Alice can't take a joke.

MRS POLSTEAD. Thing is…
 That sorta Nonsense Isn't Bloody Funny!
 If you want to drink in my pub…
 Bloody Behave!
 That's a girl! Get Out.

MEN (*leaving*). Sorry, Mrs Polstead. / Sorry, Brenda.
 No arm done just having / some fun…

7. Alice Talks

ALICE. I was *fifteen* when this – (*Air quotes.*) '*adventure*'
    kicked off,
    so old enough to… (*Holding up cigarette packet.*)
    My world was a bit *shit*… (*Lights a cigarette.*)
    My mum? Brilliant at making kids.
    Looking after em?
    Rubbish.
    Looked after my brothers and sisters until I thought…
    Sod that… only person I'm looking after from now on is *me*!
    Sod London! Went in search of adventure.
    (*Beat.*)
    But unless you got *money,* adventure ain't all it's cracked up
    to be.
    (*Beat.*)
    Old Ma Polstead found me begging down Jericho so…
    Pot girl. The Trout.
    Pot boy – (*Utter loathing.*) *Malcolm Polstead.*
    Which stinks but… better than London.

GERARD BONNEVILLE *appears from round a corner.*

BONNEVILLE. You okay?

ALICE. Me? Yeah. Why? Who are you?

BONNEVILLE. I saw what happened.

ALICE. I'm fine.
    (*Beat.*)
    Thanks.

BONNEVILLE. I'd like to apologise on behalf of my sex.
    But would you like me to go and punch their lights out?

ALICE. I'm fine.

BONNEVILLE. Sure?

ALICE. Sure.

BONNEVILLE. Thank Christ – I'm absolutely shit at physical
    combat.

ALICE. They just do it cos I ain't pretty. They think I'll be
    grateful.

BONNEVILLE (*re: cigarette*). Don't suppose you've got
a spare one of those have you?
I'm all of a tremble with being brave!

ALICE. Here. Where's your dæmon?

BONNEVILLE*'s dæmon, a* HYENA, *appears*.

Is she a…

BONNEVILLE. Hyena.

HYENA *laughs*. BEN, *as a cat who has been sniffing around
her, stiffens*.

ALICE. She *laughs*.

BONNEVILLE. She finds the world *hilarious*.
(*Strokes the* HYENA.) Don't you… you hysterical female?

HYENA *fawns*.

Actually… she's just a nervous giggler.

HYENA *giggles*.

ALICE. How'd she lose her leg?

BONNNEVILLE. Smoking.

ALICE. Liar.

BONNEVILLE. Seriously, smoking.
She has to pay for *all* my bad habits and stupid mistakes.
Don't you? You poor girl?

HYENA *laughs and imposes herself on* BEN, *who changes
shape from cat to attack dog… which snarls at* HYENA.

I see *yours* hasn't settled yet.

ALICE. He will *soon*. I'm fifteen!

BONNEVILLE. Well I hope he doesn't settle as one of these!

BEN. Me too, mate.

HYENA *laughs*. BEN *snarls*.

ALICE. *Behave*, Ben.

BONNEVILLE. Fifteen. You're very grown up for your age...
Come meet my dæmon, Ben.

BEN. I don't like new people.

ALICE. Ben don't like new people.

BONNEVILLE. Come on, Ben... talk to my dæmon.

But BEN *won't.*

ALICE. He ent much of a talker.

BONNEVILLE. The very opposite of me then... I'm a *hell* of
a talker.
Except to CCD!
Why do you think they're after Lord Nugent?

ALICE. Dunno.

BONNEVILLE. Mind you, Nugent *ent* much of a drinker...
so why was the old duffer here?
D'you suppose it's something to do with why he was sacked?

ALICE. Dunno. I just work here.

BONNEVILLE. You're not much of a talker either, are you?

MRS POLSTEAD *(distant). Alice!*

BONNEVILLE. Alice. Pretty name. Suits you.

MRS POLSTEAD *(distant). Alice!*

MALCOLM *(coming onto the terrace).* Oy! Face-ache.
Mum says take this spare bread to the nuns.

ALICE. Take it yourself, Fat Stuff!

MALCOLM. Take it, Lazy Pig!

ALICE. Least I'm not a Fat Pig!

MALCOLM *storms off, Priory direction.*

BONNEVILLE. Nice comeback!

MALCOLM *(calling back).* I'm telling Mum you won't go!

ALICE. Ooo I'm terrified!

BONNEVILLE. What a *revolting* boy.

ALICE. I hate him to *death*!
  (*Beat*.)
  I got to go.

BONNEVILLE. *Why?*

ALICE. Work.

  BONNEVILLE *follows her as…*

BONNEVILLE. Alice!

ALICE. What?

BONNEVILLE. What time do you get off?

8. Malcolm Talks to Lyra…

The Priory kitchen. LYRA *is in a big laundry basket by the kitchen stove, on which is a bubbling pot of stew.*

MALCOLM. Are we gonna take the lady's book back?

ASTA. Are we going to let her have the acorn?

MALCOLM. I don't know…
  Let's ask Lyra. Hello, Lyra.

ASTA. Hello, Pantalaimon.

MALCOLM. It's *Malcolm*.

ASTA. It's *Asta*.

MALCOLM. We met a bit ago?

ASTA. In the garden?

MALCOLM. Lot of stuff's happened to us since we met…
  CCD interrogated me!

ASTA. But they got nothing out of us!

MALCOLM. You're still top secret!

ASTA. School's got a bit weird though…

MALCOLM. There's this League of St Alexander thing…

ASTA. We're wondering about a badge…

MALCOLM. No, we're not! It's snitching.
CCD got Mr Boatwright but he *escaped*…

ASTA. *We* want to escape from Alice.

MALCOLM. We *hate* her!

FENELLA *arrives, anxious.*

Hello, Sister Fenella.

FENELLA. Malcolm! What are you doing here?

MALCOLM. Mum sent me. I used her key.

FENELLA. Guard that key with your life. There's so many
strangers knocking at our door lately…
asking their questions…
I thought you might be one of them, trying to sneak round
the back way.

MALCOLM. I got presents!
Bread for *you*. (*To* LYRA.) And for you… I made this in
woodwork a bit ago.
(*Demonstrates.*) It's a little ball of beechwood on a lanyard.

FENELLA. Ooo… a little wooden ball… for a six-month-old
baby.

MALCOLM. I sanded this myself so it's smooth for her,
so she won't get splinters or anything…
If she does swallow it by mistake, you can pull it out by
the lanyard.

FENELLA (*carefully taking the ball and lanyard from* LYRA).
It's lovely, Malcolm…

ISOBEL *arrives.*

But… here's Sister Isobel for your bath!

MALCOLM. Hello, Sister Isobel!

ISOBEL. Hello, Malcolm!

ISOBEL *takes* LYRA *and exits.*

FENELLA. Tell Sister Katherine Mrs Polstead has sent us some bread. We can have it with the oxtail stew.

MALCOLM *and* ASTA *look gutted.*

MALCOLM. You didn't give Lyra her present!

FENELLA. Silly me! I'll give it to her after her bath. (*Pockets it.*) I hope I don't forget to give it to her!

MALCOLM. It's better than a League of St Alexander badge!

FENELLA. What on earth is a League of St Alexander badge?

MALCOLM. It's this badge you get if you tell the Church about anything suspicious.
This Mrs Coulter told us / about…

FENELLA. Mrs Coulter came to your school?

MALCOLM. Yes. Why?

FENELLA. Malcolm… you won't tell Mrs Coulter about Lyra, will you?

MALCOLM. Course I won't! I promised not to tell anybody.
Why should I tell Mrs Coulter?
(*Beat.*)
Why Mrs Coulter?
What's Lyra got to do with Mrs Coulter?

FENELLA. Nothing at all!

MALCOLM. Sister Fenella…
(*Beat.*)
Is Mrs Coulter Lyra's mother?
(*Beat.*)
Mrs Coulter's Lyra's mother, isn't she?

FENELLA. No.

MALCOLM. Yes.

FENELLA. Malcolm, I wish you weren't such a clever boy!

MALCOLM. Why would she abandon her own baby?

FENELLA. Oh, this is all so bad for my ticker…

MALCOLM. Why would she abandon her own baby? (*He's not budging until he gets an answer.*)
What about her husband? Is her husband a bastard so she / had to…

FENELLA. Language, Malcolm… and… oh dear…
Should I be telling you this?
Her husband isn't Lyra's father…

MALCOLM. Who is?

FENELLA *in an agony of indecision.*

If her father's around he should be looking after her!

FENELLA. Her father is Lord Asriel so…

MALCOLM (*a bit loud*). Lord Asriel *the explorer*?

FENELLA. Ssshhh!

MALCOLM. The *Arctic* explorer who went to the Arctic in that four-rotor extreme-weather gyrocopter? *That* Lord Asriel?

FENELLA. *That* Lord Asriel, Malcolm. Mrs Coulter is –
(*Corrects herself.*) *was* a married lady.
She and Lord Asriel fell in love…
These things happen…
The ways of the flesh we must not *judge*. Mr Coulter, her lawfully married husband,
caught them together in Lord Asriel's house…
they fought to the death… well to Mr Coulter's death anyway. On the lawn!
Which in the eyes of the court was self-defence. It produced poor Lyra, born out of wedlock… Mrs Coulter abandoned her.

MALCOLM. So she doesn't know Lyra's here?

FENELLA. No, and she mustn't find out.

MALCOLM. Does Lord Asriel know?

FENELLA. No, and the court says he's not allowed within fifty miles of her, but honestly we just don't know so I beg you with all the saints to remember your most sacred promise, Malcolm!

MALCOLM. Why did Lord Nugent put her *here*?

FENELLA. We're a *sanctuarium*, Malcolm… from the Latin.
　　Any word ending in 'arium'
　　means 'a container for keeping something in'.
　　Jordan College in Oxford is a *sanctuarium scholasticorium*.
　　If you're a scholar in need, you can knock on their door, say
　　'Secundum me legem de refugia scholasticorum
　　protectionem tegimentumque huius collegii.'
　　They'll take you in.

MALCOLM. How do you know Latin, Sister Fenella?

FENELLA. I was a very bookish girl, Malcolm,
　　who wanted to join a college and read for the rest of my life.
　　But God just kept whispering in my ear 'I need you to do all
　　the heavy lifting, Fenella,'
　　so I ended up in this sanctuary *ordinarium,*
　　for *ordinary* human beings!
　　Thank your mother / for this…

MALCOLM. Remember to give Lyra her beechwood ball!

FENELLA. Well I'm very forgetful… so if I don't…
　　Babies actually like *soft* toys, Malcolm.
　　(*She exits with the bread*.)

9. St Sophia's. Hannah Relf's Rooms

MALCOLM *into* HANNAH*'s rooms at St Sophia's.*
MALCOLM *sees all the wonderful books.*
ASTA *and* JESPER, HANNAH*'s marmoset dæmon, touch*
noses.

MALCOLM. You've got a lot of books.

HANNAH. Yes.

　　She watches him looking, with envy, at all the books.

　　You like books?

MALCOLM. Yep – (*He nods and hands over her book.*) Sorry
　　it's a bit wet.

HANNAH. And the acorn?

>MALCOLM *hands her the acorn. Watches as she opens it.*
>What?

MALCOLM. I was watching to see if you knew which way it unscrewed.

JESPER. He's clever.

MALCOLM. It fooled *me* at first.

HANNAH. If I'd tried to unscrew it the wrong way…

MALCOLM. Then I wouldn't have given you the message. (*Hands her the message.*)

JESPER. And *tough*.

HANNAH (*reading it*). How did you *get* this?

MALCOLM. The man who drowned dropped it.

HANNAH. Robert Luckhurst. From Magdalen. One of us. My God!

MALCOLM. 'Us'?

HANNAH. The people who exchange information via these. It's safer if we never meet.

MALCOLM. That's a good system.

HANNAH. Malcolm, this message…
Have you made a copy of it?

MALCOLM. No –
(*Beat.*)
I just read it so much it memorised itself.
'Please enquire through the alethiometer…
If there is any connection between the particle Rusakov has discovered
and the phenomenon called *Dust*?
The other side are taking a significant interest.'
Sorry.

HANNAH. Malcolm. Don't *say* or *do* anything to link you with me, Robert Luckhurst, or this message.

MALCOLM. Okay.

HANNAH. I need a firm promise.

MALCOLM. Promise. What's an 'alethiometer'? (*Wrong pronunciation.*)

HANNAH (*corrects him*). Alethiometer.

MALCOLM. I only *read* that word… so *you're* probably right.

HANNAH. *This* is the instrument.

JESPER. Is that a good idea?

> HANNAH *takes off a black velvet cloth and reveals the beautiful alethiometer.*
> MALCOLM *loves it.*

MALCOLM. Can I touch it?

HANNAH. Of course, but be…

MALCOLM (*examines it delicately*). All these pictures… bird, hourglass, dolphin, alpha, o/mega –

HANNAH. Symbols.

MALCOLM. It's *amazing*… how does it work?

HANNAH. You ask it a question… you point the three shorter hands, see?

MALCOLM. Yes.

HANNAH. To the three symbols you *sense* might help. So I asked it to find the acorn…
Then this fourth longer hand swings where it wants to…

> MALCOLM *forensically scrutinises the fourth hand.*

Then I make my mind go clear and
(*She hands him the alethiometer and –*)
it's sort of like looking down into water.

> MALCOLM *looks.*

The clearness and understanding go so deep
you can't see the bottom… and it gave me
fish
tavern
boy…

MALCOLM. *The Trout Inn!* Me!
Does it tell the future*?*

HANNAH. It tells you the truth.

MALCOLM. Is that the only one there is?

HANNAH. There are six. Well… there *were* six… five in
universities like this one…

MALCOLM. Where's the sixth?

HANNAH. No one knows.
So the sixth may just be idle rumour.
I'm this one's keeper and suddenly rather in demand.

MALCOLM (*beat*). What's Rusakov?

HANNAH. *Who's* Rusakov… he's the man who discovered
Dust.

MALCOLM. What's Dust?

HANNAH. It's a not very good name for something that
enriches us and, in turn, is nurtured by us.

MALCOLM. Does it have anything to do with the uncertainty
principle?

HANNAH. How do you know about the uncertainty principle?

MALCOLM. I live in a pub. Near a university town. I listen.

HANNAH. Not just to scholars.

MALCOLM. To everybody.

HANNAH (*makes an unusual decision*). Malcolm. If you ever
overhear anything else that's interesting,
will you come and tell me about it?
Even if it's something different about someone you
normally trust.

ASTA *and* JESPER *register this request.*

JESPER. Are you sure about this?

ASTA. She sounds like Mrs Coulter and her League of St Alexander.

HANNAH. Anybody in the pub talking about something, anything that seems *off* to you.

ASTA. She sounds like the CCD men.

MALCOLM. Alright... how?

HANNAH. Let's employ *this* system.
She returned my book. I noticed how much you loved books, and offered to lend you mine.
You bring them back, report to me, I lend you another one –
(*Selects and hands him.*) Here's *The Body in the Library.*
It's a thriller...

JESPER. Come on, he's got a brain...

HANNAH. And this...

MALCOLM (*takes, reading*). *A Brief History of Time.*

HANNAH. Excellent! Malcolm... I'm going to have to push you out –

Steady heavy rain.

in all this *rain*!
What have we done to our climate?
This deluge is practically biblical!

They exit as...

10. The Bridge

ALICE *and* BONNEVILLE *enter together. He's covering her with his coat. The rain is stopping.*

BONNEVILLE. That Priory…?

Smiling and quite nice laughing from the HYENA.

It's actually a significant medieval building…
The oratory's supposed to be amazing…
Have you seen it, Alice?

ALICE. No.

BONNEVILLE. You've never been to the Priory?

ALICE. Oh, I've *been*. On errands for Ma Polstead.
She gives them our leftovers.
But I only go in the kitchen and that.

BONNEVILLE. This old Oxford drinking mate of mine says,
'There's these medieval floor tiles in the oratory…
go look, Gerard, they're astounding!'
I go… Nuns say 'Sorry, we're closed to visitors.'
I say 'Well, not *usually*…'
The formidable Mother Superior barks
'Well, we are today, Young Man!'
(*Beat.*)
I'm going to have to dress up as *you*, Alice, and take them
some leftovers!

ALICE, BONNEVILLE *and* HYENA *laugh at this thought.*

ALICE. Don't you think you're a bit tall to be me?

BONNEVILLE. Good point. I'll either have to go on my knees,
or think of some other way of getting past that frightening nun!
Before we're all underwater!
(*He looks down into the river…*)
Water's running very fast, isn't it? Look at the sheer *force* of it.
If it keeps on rising like this, it's going to break its banks…
do some *spectacular* damage.

ALICE. I *hate* water.

BEN *whines*.

BONNEVILLE. You hate *water*?
Why do you 'hate water', Alice Parslow?

ALICE. It's wet. And too fast. And full of things swimming in it.
In London, anyway.
I once saw something in the water below Tower Bridge...

BONNEVILLE. A *corpse*...!

ALICE. Not a corpse... something *alive*... but...
It whispered to me.

BONNEVILLE. What did it say?

ALICE. 'I know what you really are, Alice.'
(*Beat.*)
It was slimy and transparent,
and it was just waiting to reach up and pull me under...

BONNEVILLE. That's scary.

ALICE. I know.

BONNEVILLE. But you know there's lots of beings out there
that aren't scary.
They're fascinating and strange, but I can see I'm not
convincing you so
I think we should forget about scary stuff and do
something *nice*.
Let's go to the Priory, demand to see the floor tiles.

ALICE. I can't. Not now.
They'll be missing me indoors.

BONNEVILLE. But *when*, Fair Alice?

ALICE. Tomorrow?

BONNEVILLE. Tomorrow it is.
(*Beat.*)
Alice.
I won't let any slimy thing pull you underwater.

ALICE (*befuddled by* BONNEVILLE*'s attention runs
cannoning into* MALCOLM).
Get outta my way, Professor *Fatty*!
(*Exits.*)

MALCOLM. Stop calling me that! I'm not!

BONNEVILLE. Girls… more complicated than Applied
Metaphysics!

MALCOLM. Sorry… I'm… canoe.

*The sky has cleared. He wants to get in his canoe, go for
a trip on his own.*

Sorry.

ASTA. Look at his dæmon! She's *giggling*.

BONNEVILLE. Poor pot boy.

MALCOLM. *Malcolm Polstead.*

BONNEVILLE. *Malcolm Polstead*. Sorry, Malcolm.
Puberty… nightmare… right?

MALCOLM *doesn't answer*.

Your head and your body suddenly fighting each other?

MALCOLM *doesn't answer*.

Driving you *berserk*, right?

MALCOLM. No.

BONNEVILLE. Don't worry… it all gets better.
You come through the fog, the mist clears, your dæmon
settles,
the turmoil waging war in your pants finally makes a peace
treaty with your brain,
and you suddenly understand that girls are actually rather
wonderful,
and what you want most in all the world.
Then it all gets very interesting.
Shhh!

Both listen… the sound of a motorboat.

A CCD patrol boat!

Torches far off.

CCD land patrol! Pincer movement!
Some poor bastard's for it tonight!

It's not going to be *this* poor bastard!
(*He pushes* MALCOLM *off from the bank*.)
Off you go, Malcolm!
Illigitimi non carborundum!
Don't let the bastards grind you down!

He exits, leaving MALCOLM *under the amazing night sky in his canoe*.

ASTA. What he just said about the war in your pants…

MALCOLM. We're not thinking about that now!

ASTA. Got you.
(*Beat*.)
CCD's busy tonight!

MALCOLM. Very busy. Is the patrol boat moving up or downstream?

ASTA. S'not moving. It's over the other bank with all its lights off.

MALCOLM. That's unusual. Where's the land patrol?

ASTA. Looks like they're heading towards the Priory…

MALCOLM. We need to get inside, warn the sisters to hide Lyra…

11. A Father

MALCOLM *gets out of his canoe at the Priory. As CCD lights search the night, he is suddenly seized from behind. A* SNOW LEOPARD DÆMON *pins* ASTA.

ASRIEL (*low voice*). Don't struggle or you'll break your arm.

MALCOLM *stills*.

I've been watching. You visit the Priory.
The nuns are refusing others entry, but they let *you* in.
Nod if that is true.

MALCOLM *nods*.

Is there a baby there?

MALCOLM *stays still*.

Yes or no?

MALCOLM *stays still*.

That's neither no nor yes.
Is there a baby in the Priory?

MALCOLM *shakes his head*.

You are an honest boy. Your head says 'no', but your pulse tells me 'yes'.
I don't particularly *like* killing people, but I will kill *you* if you don't tell me the truth.
Is there a baby in the Priory?
Don't leave your poor mother without a son...

MALCOLM *reluctantly nods*.

That's better. Nod if that baby's name is Lyra.

MALCOLM *nods*.

And her dæmon is Pantalaimon. Behold the snow leopard who gave her that name.

The SNOW LEOPARD *acknowledges this somehow*.

ASTA. It's *Lord Asriel*.

ASRIEL. I see you've heard of me.
You probably know I shouldn't be within fifty miles of here.
I need you to wake up the nuns so I can speak to them and
it's *urgent*.
(*Takes his hand from* MALCOLM*'s mouth.*)

MALCOLM (*whisper*). I'm not going to take you to the / nuns!

ASRIEL (*low voice*). Yes you are. Walk.
(*Starts frog-marching* MALCOLM *towards the Priory.*)

MALCOLM (*dragged along*). What's urgent? Is Lyra in
danger?

ASRIEL. Yes.

MALCOLM (*yanked forward*). Who from? Why *urgent*?

They are at the Priory.

ASRIEL. Wake them up! *Wake them up!*

MALCOLM. Reverend Mother! Wake up! You got to wake up!
You got a visitor!
Reverend Mother! Sister Fenella! Anybody?

NUNS *arrive, woken from their sleep.*

ANNE. Is it trouble? Is it the / police?

FENELLA. Is it Malcolm? That's Malcolm's voice, / isn't it?

ASRIEL. I'm Asriel. I am the father of the baby you have here…
No point denying it… I've forced this boy to admit it.
I need to see she is still alive.

BENEDICTA. I'm afraid that will not be possible. She's under /
my care.

ASRIEL. I'm not here to take her away. I'm not here to do her
harm.

NUNS *don't move.*

Bring her to me.

NUNS *don't move.*

Don't make me hurt the boy.

He takes hold of MALCOLM*'s arm until…*

BENEDICTA. Sister Fenella, fetch the child.

FENELLA *goes to get* LYRA.

ASRIEL. Reverend Mother, I believe she is in danger from her mother, Marisa Coulter, who gave her up, but is now taking an *enormous* interest in her.

BENEDICTA. Surely that is a *good* thing…

ASRIEL. It is *not*. This is *not* late-arriving maternal love. Witches in Sweden…

BENEDICTA (*she doesn't hold with witches*). Witches?

ASRIEL. Witches in Sweden have heard voices in the aurora prophesying great change, as a result of which, Lyra's mother and others…

BENEDICTA. Others?

ASRIEL. The Magisterium, Reverend Mother, think our child is the subject of that prophecy,
and therefore of immense value.
I believe Marisa will come and claim her and then hand her to the Magisterium.
Don't indulge her.

BENEDICTA (*lifts her hand*). As God is my witness, we will not be handing the child to anyone at all.

FENELLA *returns with* LYRA.

ASRIEL. Is this her, boy?

MALCOLM. Yes, and it's actually *Malcolm Polstead*.

ASRIEL. I'm satisfied. Thank you, Reverend Mother.
(*He's about to go. Job done.*)

FENELLA. Lord Asriel, you might like to hold her just *the once*. Here…

And hands him the baby in such a way he has to take her.

There you go… just a few seconds. So you know each other *a bit*…

ASRIEL *takes* LYRA. *Everybody watches… concerned.*
He walks a little way away from them all as…

BENEDICTA. Sister Fenella… was that wise?

FENELLA. Who cares? He *made* her, he should know what not keeping it in his trousers *means*.

ANNE. Where's he taking her?

BENEDICTA. Off! He's taking her *off*!

FENELLA. Just into the *garden*, Mother.

ANNE. What's he doing?

FENELLA. He's *looking* at her!

He is. He's finding her absolutely fascinating.

BENEDICTA. Is she crying?

ANNE. No. She's…

FENELLA. Trying to *talk* to him…

ASRIEL lifts LYRA up to the moon.

BENEDICTA. Oh he's lifting her up!

ANNE. The heathen's sacrificing her!

FENELLA. No… he's showing her *the moon*!

CCD lights get closer.

MALCOLM. Lord Asriel! CCD! You got to go!

ASRIEL brings LYRA back.

ASRIEL. She likes the moon! And she seems remarkably content about the havoc she will wreak on the earth below! (*Gives her to* FENELLA.)

FENELLA. So… that's your *daddy*… what did you think of him? She says 'You're very handsome.'

The CCD are heard nearer.

MALCOLM. Lord Asriel. *Come on!*

BENEDICTA. Inside, sisters.

The NUNS take LYRA and exit.

MALCOLM. I don't suppose your four-rotor extreme-weather gyrocopter is / around, is it?

ASRIEL. Sadly in *Greenwich*, Malcolm Polstead.

MALCOLM. Quick! You can go down Godstow Road.

Lights appear before them on the road.

ASRIEL. No good! More of them on the road. Over the bridge! I could hide in the pub.

MALCOLM. You're not putting my mum in danger!

ASRIEL. Then I'll have to swim.

MALCOLM. River's too fast.

ASRIEL. I'll have to chance it.

MALCOLM (*huge sacrifice*). You better take my canoe…

ASTA. MALCOLM!

MALCOLM. Go downriver. Get in!

ASRIEL *gets into the canoe.* SNOW LEOPARD *leaps in, ears flat.*

Paddle is under the…

ASRIEL *finds a paddle.*

ASRIEL. Thank you, Malcolm Polstead! Keep an eye on my daughter!
(*Floating fast downstream.*) Don't let this fine clear night fool you.
In a few days, the rain's coming back even harder.
Things have been disturbed in the water,
and there'll be the biggest flood for a hundred years.
And this country will *suffer*. Be ready.
(*Paddles.*) This is a good canoe! I'll get her back to you!

Searchlights.

MALCOLM. Look after her!
(*Watches* ASRIEL *go.*) Poor Lyra!
(*Thinks about* ASRIEL.) Some father!

ASTA. Some mother!

MALCOLM. Yeh. Her *father* was right about the weather!
Three nights of this big red moon!
Three days of weird bright glaring baking sun, then...

Lightning, thunder, then cloudburst. It rains steadily into...

And at school...

School gathers.

First our headmaster disappeared, no warning, then
suddenly...

12. St Alexander Continues to Cleanse

TEACHERS *in silent terror before* ERIC, ROBBIE *and other
pupils – all wearing badges of the League of St Alexander
except for* MALCOLM, ANDREW *and* ERIC.

ERIC. Miss Dukes and Mrs Savery have something to say to
the assembled pupils of Ulvercote Elementary School –
(*Before* MISS DUKES.) Tell the League of St Alexander
you're sorry.

MISS DUKES. I'm truly sorry that I started a lesson without
a prayer.

ERIC (*before* MRS SAVERY). Tell the League of St Alexander
you're sorry.

MRS SAVERY. I'm truly sorry.

ERIC. Why are you sorry?

MRS SAVERY (*treading carefully*). I told off three members of
the League of Alexander.

ERIC. *St* Alexander.

MRS SAVERY. *St* Alexander.
(*Beat.*)
I acknowledge that I was wrong to tell off three members of
the League of...

ERIC. *St* / Alexander.

MRS SAVERY. St Alexander for what I thought was bad
behaviour during a lesson.
(*Beat*.)
I realise it was a perfectly justified discussion about the
importance of trusting in religious truth rather than the
unsubstantiated claims of science.

ERIC (*to* TEACHERS). Dismissed.

TEACHERS *file out. Everybody loves this.*

You *still* not wearing your badge, Polstead?

MALCOLM. Andrew's not wearing one.

ERIC. Yeah well, he'd better, hadn't you, Whicher?

ANDREW. Or else *what*, Eric?

ERIC. Or else I'll report you.

ANDREW. Why don't you do that, Eric, see what happens!

He squares up to ERIC, *eyeball to eyeball. Stand-off until –*

MALCOLM (*to* ERIC). *You're* not wearing your badge.

ANDREW. Leave it, Malcolm…

ERIC. That what you *think,* Polstead?
(*Turns back his lapel, reveals his badge.*) Hello? St
Alexander!

MALCOLM. Why're you hiding it?

ERIC. I've reached *second-degree* St Alexander.

MALCOLM. What does *that* mean?

ERIC. It means I can keep an eye on people, and they don't
know…

MALCOLM. That's pathetic.

ERIC (*punch*). Wear your badge, Polstead!

ROBBO (*punch*). Join the League of St Alexander, St Andrew.

School dissolves, each of the League of St Alexander giving MALCOLM *and* ANDREW *a warning punch, which they receive stoically.* FLORA *seizes* MALCOLM*'s bag, empties it on the floor:* HANNAH*'s books, school stuff, and his old teddy bear, David, fall out.*

RUBY. Ooo… Polstead's got a teddy bear!

MALCOLM. It's a present for somebody!

ROBBO. *Badge*, Polstead!

ANDREW. Alright, Malcolm.

MALCOLM. Alright.

ASTA. Don't cry till they've gone.

MALCOLM. I'm not.

ASTA. We need to learn boxing.

Once the others have gone, MALCOLM *starts repacking his bag.*

MALCOLM. School used to feel *safe*.

ASTA. Want to let it all out now?

MALCOLM. No.
(*He's holding* HANNAH*'s books.*)
The Body in the Library and *A Brief History of Time*.
We should just take these books back to Professor Relf…

13. St Sophia's College

HANNAH *is putting the alethiometer back in its black velvet cloth.* MRS COULTER *is pacing and frustrated.*

HANNAH. I'm sorry the reading was so unhelpful, Mrs Coulter.

MRS COULTER. I'm sorry too.

HANNAH. The alethiometer always tells the truth, but it leaves *you* to catch up with it.
Be patient, Mrs Coulter.
Eventually, a sort of light comes on in your mind and you think 'Ah, I understand now.'

MALCOLM *enters.*

MRS COULTER. My search is urgent, Dr Relf.
I can't enjoy the *luxury* of patience.

HANNAH (*sees* MALCOLM). Oh. Malcolm. Hello.
We were just discussing the awfulness of St Sophia's food.
(*To* MRS COULTER.) This is my friend Malcolm.
(*To* MALCOLM.) Malcolm. Mrs Coulter. A *brilliant* star in the St Sophia firmament.
One of our most distinguished graduates.

MRS COULTER. Malcolm, hello.

MRS COULTER *holds out her hand.* MALCOLM *avoids taking it.*
Her GOLDEN MONKEY *notices and approaches* MALCOLM.

MALCOLM. Hello.

MRS COULTER (*lightly touches* MALCOLM*'s blazer pocket badge*). This is an Ulvercote Elementary School blazer, isn't it?
What are you doing so far from rural Ulvercote, Malcolm?

MALCOLM. Nothing. Just visiting.

MRS COULTER. How *on earth* do you two know each other?

MALCOLM. We just ran into each / other once…

HANNAH. Malcolm lives at The Trout Inn. I sometimes go there on warm evenings for a drink.
And I left my book there. And Malcolm very kindly returned it to me!

MRS COULTER. What a gentleman!

HANNAH. Now I lend him books.

MALCOLM (*taking out his two books*). Here. Brought these back. Thank you.

MRS COULTER. The Trout? Isn't that the inn at Godstow?

HANNAH. On the river, yes.

MRS COULTER. I think I *know* it. Isn't it the one across from St Rosamund's Priory?

HANNAH (*simultaneous*). Yes.

MALCOLM (*simultaneous*). Well not straight across.

The GOLDEN MONKEY *is very interested in* MALCOLM.

MRS COULTER (*beat*). Do you ever visit the Priory, Malcolm?

MALCOLM. Not really.

MRS COULTER. 'Not really.' What does that mean?

MALCOLM. I don't *visit*. I just take my mum's leftovers to the nuns sometimes.

MRS COULTER. What a kind boy!
(*Leaving*.) Dr Relf, you two have books to swap. I shan't outstay my welcome.

HANNAH. I'm sorry my reading wasn't more helpful.

MRS COULTER. Don't worry, Dr Relf.
Everything has been most illuminating. Goodbye, Hannah. Goodbye, Malcolm.
(*Exits with her* GOLDEN MONKEY.)

MALCOLM. What did *she* want?

HANNAH. 'She' is a rather brilliant scientist who wanted me to consult the alethiometer…

MALCOLM. What did you ask it?

HANNAH. She wanted to know the current location of the baby daughter she had to give up.

MALCOLM. Did it answer?

HANNAH. It just said 'boy'. What happened? What did I do?

MALCOLM. I just told her I *do* visit the nuns!
(*He realises with horror what this means.*)
Mrs Coulter's *Lyra's* mum, she's *Magisterium* and she comes to *schools* and makes everything upside down and she's going to do something bad to Lyra.

HANNAH. Lyra...?

MALCOLM. Her *baby*!

HANNAH. *Sorry*, her *baby*.

MALCOLM. Then you ask me to spy for you, *you* tell me to trust *you* and report to *you* and I ent got nobody else I can trust except my mum and I don't want to get *her* in trouble because...
okay...
last night Lord Asriel leaps on me out of the dark and says 'I'll kill you!'

HANNAH. *Asriel?*

MALCOLM. But then I trusted him *anyway* and then *CCD* arrived and I even gave him *my Albion oak-bark canoe* which he'll probably just think 'pointless scuzzy old *kayak*' and sink it, but anyway *he* tells the sisters not to trust Lyra's mother your *college* friend there, but I arrive and you're giving her alethiometer readings... so... okay... Lord Asriel and Mrs Coulter's baby is hidden in the Priory at Godstow but I was supposed to keep that secret but what's the point cos you've told her I live at The Trout and I'm clearly *a boy* and she's gonna put it all together and now I got Lyra in Serious Danger!
(*Beat.*)
Here's your books back. *The Body in the Library* was *great* but I read *A Brief History of Time* and found it *very hard-going*.
(*Beat.*)
Sorry!

HANNAH. Don't be sorry. *I'm* sorry.
(*Beat*.)
I don't understand *A Brief History of Time* either.
(*Beat*.)
I've put you and…

MALCOLM. *Lyra*.

HANNAH. In danger.
Lyra is clearly part of some power struggle between her parents and I need to contact Lord Nugent and find out *why*. Malcolm, I'm sorry.

Oxford clock tower strikes.

MALCOLM. I'll go warn the nuns!

HANNAH. Malcolm, I'm so sorry.

And both exit as…

14. In the Ashmolean Museum

BONNEVILLE *approaches* NUGENT. NUGENT *doesn't like this at all*.

BONNEVILLE. Thomas Nugent. Congratulations.
The new Master of Jordan College.

NUGENT. Gerard Bonneville… a free man again.

BONNEVILLE. Jordan being the only college which grants scholastic sanctuary, and you being its Master, Thomas…

The HYENA *flattens and abases*.

'*Secundum me legem de refugia scholasticorum protectionem tegimentumque huius collegii*.'

NUGENT. *Sanctuary*, Gerard? Superfluous surely? You served your time.

BONNEVILLE. You're also working *against* the government now they've sacked you…

NUGENT. I really can't be seen with you, Gerard.
And I have a meeting in…

BONNEVILLE. That's why I'm ambushing you in the
Ashmolean, Thomas!
(*Beat*.)
I need just two minutes of your time.
(*Beat*.)
Dare me due minut-es tempus tuam.

NUGENT. Two minutes.
(*Checks his watch. He means two minutes*.)

BONNEVILLE. You know I've been working on Dust, /
Thomas.

NUGENT. I know you were convicted of abusing young
children, / Gerard.

BONNEVILLE. *Girls*, they were *girls* not *child/ren*…

NUGENT. And there are other scholars working on Dust.
Asriel's taking an interest, and Marisa / Coulter…

BONNEVILLE. That *moist whore's* a fine one to be swanning
about symposiums on experimental theology, talking so
brilliantly about *scholastic purity*, while fornicating with
Asriel on every flat surface in England!

NUGENT. For which she's paid a huge price. *She* lost all *her*
research funds just as you did.

BONNEVILLE. And she's now ingratiating herself with the
Magisterium to get them back!
Thomas… you need to get ahead of them!
I am your best hope! *I* am the person in this world
closest to understanding what Dust *is* and what it *does*.
I have not wasted my time in my lonely prison cell…
I've thought and worked night and day
to develop a theory infinitely more advanced than
Rusakov's!
I think I've nailed it. Let me show you my notes!
(*Gestures to notes in his bag*.)

NUGENT (*clicks his watch*). One minute, Gerard.

BONNEVILLE. The Magisterium have Coulter. You could have me…
the brightest and *best*, Thomas… I can tell you *what Dust means*,
and it will *revolutionise* our understanding of matter.
The way we see the world will be *forever* changed,
the Magisterium will become irrelevant,
and its power will melt away like snow in August.

NUGENT. And your price, Gerard?

BONNEVILLE. *Funds!*
A decent research fellowship here in Oxford… Jordan would be ideal!
Nobody could touch me there!
But I'd settle for anywhere with lab access and a decent research team.
Dear Old Friend. Let me back inside!

HANNAH *arrives in the background. Sees* NUGENT *is with* BONNEVILLE. *Waits, watching.*

NUGENT. I'm sorry, Gerard. I'm powerless.

BONNEVILLE. *Untrue!*

NUGENT. I've been kicked out of of/fice.

BONNEVILLE. And become the secret opposition.

NUGENT. Sorry I can't help you.

BONNEVILLE. *Won't* help me.

NUGENT. *Can't.*

BONNEVILLE. Don't believe you.

NUGENT. Believe it. This government have cut my balls off.
I'm a neutered Tom.

BONNEVILLE (*stands and blocks* NUGENT). Just some *funds* and *access*, Thomas.

NUGENT. That's enough, Gerard!
(*Beat.*)
Maybe in a few years…

when memories have faded, when the 'dust' has settled.
I'm afraid you are currently just too toxic.

BONNEVILLE *seizes his lapels*. LEMUR *alerts*. HYENA
rises up.
HANNAH *comes forward to intervene as…*

Let me go, Bonneville. *This* is why we can't trust you.
You're as unstable as you are toxic.

HANNAH. Is everything alright here?

NUGENT. Everything's *fine*.

BONNEVILLE. Everything's *not* fine! (*He releases* NUGENT.)
Hannah Relf!

HANNAH. Dr Bonneville.

BONNEVILLE. *She's* your meeting? *She's the resistance?* The
slowest alethiometer reader in the world?

HANNAH. But by far the most accurate, and *reliable* around
young students.

HYENA *laughs*.

BONNEVILLE. What are *you* laughing at?
(*He hits her.*)

HANNAH. You can't hit her! She's your *dæmon*!

HYENA *cowers and continues to laugh desperately as*
BONNEVILLE *beats her*.

BONNEVILLE. You think it's funny? You think this is *funny*?
Stop laughing, you hysterical bitch!

NUGENT. Bonneville! A man doesn't attack his own dæmon!
He might as well cut out his own heart.

BONNEVILLE. He does when he is cheated of his destiny.
I am the man who will show the world what Dust *is*.
If you won't help me, I'll find someone who will.

HYENA *laughs*.

Walk, you hysterical bitch!

BONNEVILLE *drags* HYENA *off by her ear.* NUGENT *and* HANNAH *pat or stroke their* DÆMONS. *Dæmons and humans alike shocked rigid.*

HANNAH. Gerard Bonneville?

NUGENT. Gerard Bonneville. Unravelling.
    (*Beat.*)
    I got your note, Dr Relf, but as you have just seen
    this is neither a good time or / place…

HANNAH. I need to know why the baby you gave to the nuns
    at Godstow is so important.

NUGENT. I can't tell you that, Dr Relf.

HANNAH. I know the child is Lord Asriel's daughter.
    Lord Nugent, he's visited her.
    Marisa Coulter came to my college, asking me to ask the
    alethiometer to find her baby. And I think she now knows her
    whereabouts.

NUGENT. You have no idea what you've done.

He tries to leave. She stops him.

HANNAH. Lord Nugent, *please*… I've turned this boy into
    a spy. How do we keep him safe?

NUGENT. We don't.
    The baby is important, Dr Relf. The boy is not.

They leave together.

15. The Priory

Heavy rain pours. MALCOLM *runs across the bridge, carrying the teddy bear.*

ASTA. Slow down!

MALCOLM. We can't! We got to warn the nuns! And take this 'soft toy' *for Lyra*.
Because apparently she don't like little beechwood balls!

ASTA. You'll *fall*!

MALCOLM. I won't!

ASTA. I wish we still had a canoe!

MALCOLM. Lord Asriel *said* he'd return it!

ASTA. Posh people never keep their promises!

> *He runs into the Priory kitchen.* ALICE *is there with a basket of apples.*

MALCOLM. What are *you* doing here?

ALICE. Your mum sent me with the apples.
I don't know what's going on.
The CCD are here with some uppity bitch and the nuns are shitting themselves!
Shhhh! Listen!

> *They both listen until* MRS COULTER, *two* CCD HEAVIES *and the frightened* NUNS *enter.*

BENEDICTA. The storm's getting nearer, Mrs Coulter. Soon it will be right overhead.
I'm so sorry you came out on a wild goose chase.

MRS COULTER (*seeing* MALCOLM). Ah, Malcolm!
Two encounters in twenty-four hours.
What an extraordinary coincidence.
With a teddy bear? For a baby, Malcolm?
But, there's *no baby here*, is there, Reverend Mother?

> *Lightning. Then a clap of thunder.*

BENEDICTA. Someone has fed you misinformation. There's no baby here, Mrs Coulter.

MRS COULTER. Then why has Malcolm brought you a teddy bear, Reverend Mother?

Awkward silence. Filled by a gathering communal lie…

BENEDICTA. For the same reason as Alice here brought the lovely apples…

ALICE. His mum sent me with these.

BENEDICTA. The people hereabouts are so kind and charitable…
They bring us their surplus food and old toys.

FENELLA. We *do* sometimes get distressed girls –

All NUNS *nod helpfully.*

– who have got themselves in the family way…

MALCOLM (*holding out teddy bear*). This is *David*. I've outgrown him
and my mum said 'It is better to give than receive, Malcolm', so…

BENEDICTA. 'For I was hungry and you gave me food;
I was thirsty and you gave me drink;
I was a stranger and you took me in.'
Matthew twenty-five, verse thirty-five.
Mrs Coulter, I wonder if your informant has put two and two together to make five?

FENELLA. Will I take you and show you our relief chest?
Where we keep the old toys?
It's in the western vestibule…

BENEDICTA (*tries to usher them out*). I can show it to you on your way out…

MRS COULTER *and her* GOLDEN MONKEY *slowly walk towards the exit.*

You see! No baby.

Everybody watches. She's reluctantly about to leave when
LYRA *cries from oven. Everybody freezes.*

MRS COULTER. Then what on earth can that be?
(*Walks to.*) In the oven. A mouse?
(*She opens the oven door.*)
Why it's *a baby*!

She looks triumphantly at the SISTERS. *Horrible pause.*
Until ALICE *comes forward and picks* LYRA *up.*

ALICE. I'm sorry, Reverend Mother...
I should have *told* you I put her in here.

MRS COULTER. In the oven?

ALICE. Of course in the oven!

BENEDICTA. Of course in the oven! Tell us why the oven,
Alice...

ALICE. She's *my* little gel. *Ellie.*
She's a very poor sleeper, isn't she, Sister Fenella?

FENELLA. Yes. Oh yes.

ALICE. She needs complete dark.

FENELLA. Yes.

ALICE. And she sleeps best in a confined space.

FENELLA. Yes. She does. In a confined space.

ALICE. Stop your racket. Mummy's here now.

All can see she's very adept with LYRA.

MRS COULTER. Why didn't you mention this before?

ALICE. You frightened me to death! When I come in...
I thought you was *Child Protection*. I thought you'd take her
off me.
And I couldn't bear anyone to take her off me.

MRS COULTER. Is this true, Reverend Mother?

BENEDICTA. Well, of course it is!

FENELLA. Would you *ever* remember to tell us when you put your baby in the oven, Alice?
We could have roasted the little dote!

BENEDICTA (*takes her arm*). Mrs Coulter, Alice is such a *good* mother for one so young...
She's doing her best.

ALICE. I am.

BENEDICTA. I ask you, in God's name, show this troubled girl your mercy.
Please don't take her baby away. You can see how they love one another!
(*Beat.*)
Such commendable mercy. Our Heavenly Father himself thanks you. *Thank you.*
(*She presses* MRS COULTER*'s arm gratefully.*)
Let me show you and your gentlemen out.

The GOLDEN MONKEY *looks about. Something's going on but he cannot work out what.*
BENEDICTA *leads* MRS COULTER *out.* CCD MEN *follow.*
All liars still present listen like hawks.

ALICE (*whisper*). Anybody gonna tell me whose bleeding baby this is?

MALCOLM (*whisper*). We can't tell you!

NUNS. Ssssh! *SSSSSHHHH!*

And no breathing until BENEDICTA *returns.*

BENEDICTA. They've gone.

FENELLA. Who in God's name did put her in the oven?

BENEDICTA. *I* did, Sister Fenella. Perhaps not my best idea. I was somewhat *rushed.*
We are not going to discuss it further. Alice, tonight –
(*Holy finger.*)
God reaches down and places a holy kiss on your forehead for how you just saved this innocent baby!

Everybody finally breathes out...

FENELLA (*holding her heart*). Oh. My heart. Oh Jesus, Mary
and Joseph!

SISTERS *crowd round her*.

MALCOLM. Everything's alright, Sister Fenella...

ISOBEL. *Breathe*, Sister Fenella...

ALICE (*takes over, very nursey, hand on* FENELLA*'s forehead,
etc*.). She's white as paper! She's got the same thing as my
grandma.
You need to get her to bed with two aspirins
and a cup of sweet tea and a hot-water bottle.

ISOBEL *helps* FENELLA *out, then*...

You too, Reverend Mother... you had a shock *too*,
and pardon me but you're no spring chicken either!
Listen, *I'm* wide awake, Reverend Mother. I'll stay look
after Ellie.

MALCOLM. *Lyra*. I'll stay and look after her...

ALICE. Know how to change her, do you?

MALCOLM. No.

ALICE. Know how to heat her bottle to the right temperature,
do you?

MALCOLM. No but I could...

ALICE. 'Learn', Professor...? Right! *I'll* look after her. You *go
home*.
Reverend Mother, he'll get her nappy all wrong or scald her
with hot milk or something!
I'll be in charge here. Alright, Reverend Mother?

BENEDICTA. I think that is an excellent plan.

Thunder, lightning.

Malcolm, the rain has washed away the bridge at Swinford.
God knows what it will do next!
Your mother will be anxious about you... go home –
(*Beat*.)
Now!

MALCOLM *exits reluctantly*.

Thank you, Alice. What a kind, good, resourceful girl you are.

She kisses ALICE *on the top of her head. Exits*. ALICE *puts* LYRA *down*.
Goes to the edge of the space.

BEN. Don't. Don't!

ALICE. Shut up. (*Calls*.) I'm in the kitchen.

And BONNEVILLE *enters*.

BONNEVILLE. Well… this isn't where the tiles are, Alice.
(*Sees* LYRA. *Mild interest*.)
Alice, have you been keeping things from me? Is this your secret baby?

HYENA *giggles*.

ALICE. She's secret. But she's not my baby. The nuns been hiding her.

BONNEVILLE. Have they?
(*To* LYRA.) Hello, whoever you are!

ALICE. She's called Lyra.
This woman called Coulter just came to get her, but we fooled her.

BONNEVILLE. Coulter? Fascinating. No… this isn't your baby. Your baby would be much prettier.

She comes to him. They are about to kiss. MALCOLM *enters*.

MALCOLM. River is rising and rising. I need to warn the nuns.
(*Sees* BONNEVILLE.) What are you doing here?

BONNEVILLE. Well… I *was* about to turn Alice from a girl into a woman.
But you've ruined the romantic atmosphere so…
(*To* LYRA.) I guess I'll just take *you* instead as a consolation prize.
You're the reason Thomas Nugent has been visiting this *sanctuarium ordinarium*.
You're my little bargaining chip, aren't you?

ALICE. What you talking about?

BONNEVILLE. Marisa Coulter's baby. You've found her for me.
Thank you, Alice!
She's going to Switzerland with me.
Aren't you Lyra whatever-your-name-is? I'll give you to the
Magisterium.

MALCOLM (*to* ALICE). See what you done?

BONNEVILLE. I've no idea why they're so interested in you,
but you're bound to secure me a nice little research
scholarship in Geneva.

ALICE. Was this why you was nice to me? Just to get to *her*?

BONNEVILLE. Oh, not just to get to her.

A low insistent rumbling.

What's *that*?

They listen. It gets louder, more insistent.

Is it an earthquake?

MALCOLM. It's the river.

A mighty crash.

I think it's just broken its banks…

The storm is right overhead.

BONNEVILLE. Oh Alice… the water's coming to get you…
All those horrible slimy things in the water coming to get you!

And sounds of wood bending and straining.

It's coming for the Priory too!

Roof begins to fall.

The flood's coming to take us all… saints and sinners alike!

The roof cracks and screams.

Oh this is *fantastic*…

ALICE *seizes* LYRA.

ALICE (*to* BONNEVILLE). I hope you drown! I hope things in the water *eat you*!
(*She runs with* LYRA *in her arms*.)

BONNEVILLE. Alice… leave the baby! Don't take that baby… I'm warning you…

MALCOLM (*body-charges* BONNEVILLE). No, *I'm* warning *you*!

MALCOLM *and* ALICE *run outside*.
NUGENT *and* HANNAH *are running towards them over the bridge*.

HANNAH. Malcolm! Bring us the baby!

NUGENT. Quickly, boy!

The river overflows its banks. The bridge collapses, taking NUGENT *and* HANNAH *away with it*.

ALICE. The bridge just went! We're going to have to go the long way round.

MALCOLM. No! Come on! We should swim!

ALICE. I'm not going in no river!

Then, MALCOLM *sees his canoe floating towards him on the flood*.

MALCOLM. *La Belle Sauvage*! He *did* sent it back! Get in!

ALICE. Take her then!

MALCOLM. I can't take her and paddle too!

ALICE *hands* LYRA *to* MALCOLM. ALICE *gets in the canoe*.

ALICE. Give her to me! Quick!

MALCOLM *hands her* LYRA.

Get in!

As MALCOLM *gets in the canoe,* BONNEVILLE *wades through the flood towards them.*
The HYENA *in pursuit, laughing.*

He's coming! Let's go!

BONNEVILLE *staggers towards them and grabs the canoe.*

MALCOLM. Let go of my canoe. *Let go!*

HYENA *laughs.*

BONNEVILLE. Nobody's going anywhere until you give me back that baby...

MALCOLM. Let go!

MALCOLM *brings the paddle down on* BONNEVILLE*'s fingers.*
BONNEVILLE *screams in pain and lets go.*

Sorry but sorry!

BONNEVILLE *is swept out of sight by the flood.*
La Belle Sauvage *rises as the flood rises.*
The Priory roof falls in.
The flood is now high and strong. The canoe rises with the flood.
Big pieces of masonry fly past.

ALICE. What are you waiting for?
Go!

The canoe is swept downstream.

ACT TWO

1. Knowledge is Like Water

MALCOLM, ALICE *and* LYRA *in the canoe. Terrified, angry, cold and soaking.*
It is night. The water is at the height of trees, the flooded river streaming all around them.

MALCOLM. I can't see a thing!

ALICE. Get us to dry land!

MALCOLM. There isn't any!

Something bumps the canoe. ALICE *tries to see what it was.*

ALICE. *What was that?*

MALCOLM. Don't lean to one side.

Things float past, not human… there are sounds that make no sense.

ALICE. Something's crying!

MALCOLM. Don't listen!

Canoe twists and turns in the current. More strange and unsettling detritus streams past and around the canoe.

ALICE. There's *things* in the water!

MALCOLM. Don't look!

ALICE *closes her eyes.*

More sounds that make no sense… BONNEVILLE*'s* HYENA *laughing…* ALICE *opens her eyes.*

ALICE. What was that?

MALCOLM. Don't listen!

ALICE. Something laughing!

MALCOLM. I said 'don't listen!'

ALICE. *Go left, go left!*

MALCOLM. Don't tell me what to do! We wouldn't be in this if it wasn't for you and him!

ALICE. Oh right you gonna make all this my fault! TREES!

And they both have to avoid treetops.
A thorn-laden branch lashes MALCOLM *across the face.*

MALCOLM. Owwww!

ALICE. Serves you right!
(*Points.*) Water's calmer to the right! Steer us *there.*

They make it into less rapid currents. The canoe moves less and so do the unsettling things floating in the water.

I can hear things crying underwater.
(*Then she sees.*)
No!

Floating and circling, dull, soft, half-submerged… the body of a dead woman.

It's a woman.
(*Looks for –*)
No dæmon.

BEN/ASTA. No dæmon!

BEN. She's dead.

ALICE (*scared but brave*). We should pull her out.

MALCOLM. We can't. Canoe's not big enough.

They watch, very frightened, as the corpse bumps the canoe and the current makes it circle the canoe as if it is trying to board. ALICE *and* MALCOLM *moan with terror.*

ASTA. What happens to us dæmons when you lot die?

BEN. Shut up.

MALCOLM. Dunno.

Beat. This is unbearably frightening for all of them.
ASTA *crawls into* MALCOLM*'s arms,*
BEN *snuggles against* ALICE.

Maybe her dæmon was really *small.*

ASTA. Maybe…

MALCOLM. Like *a robin* or something.

ALICE. And he's in her pocket…

BEN. Shut up.

ASTA. Let's not think about it!

Beat.

MALCOLM. I can't help it.
Knowledge is like water.
It always finds gaps to leak through.

ALICE/BEN. *Shut up, Professor!*

ALICE. Current's getting faster.

MALCOLM. Don't *lean*!

The current sweeps them off and away.

2. Westminster

MRS COULTER *and* GOVERNMENT OFFICIALS *in dark suits listen to an emissary from the Magisterium in Geneva –* MICHAEL WHARTON, *Chairman of the Committee for the Propagation of the True Faith. Although he is mild and gentle, nobody dares speak.*

WHARTON. *This* is the woman who did wrong?

MRS COULTER. I know I sinned, sir.

WHARTON. Your sin produced a child which could smash the Magisterium's holy teaching to pieces.
Your sin.

MRS COULTER. I ceased for the shortest time to be alert to evil. A single mistake.

WHARTON. Not a single mistake, madam. You also, like your fellow adulterer,
pursued your investigation of 'Dust' long after we advised you not to.

MRS COULTER. Because I believed it would benefit you, sir.

WHARTON. The Magisterium does not tolerate people who make mistakes, / Mrs Coulter.

MRS COULTER. Unlike Lord Asriel, I am making reparation. My League of St Alexander persuades / young hearts…

WHARTON. Shh, shh. We gave you considerable resources because you assured us
that you would deliver your child up to our care
yet our sources tell us you found the child at Godstow Priory
and let it slip from your hands?

MRS COULTER. Forgive me, sir. I trusted the word of holy nuns.

WHARTON. Our Bible tells us –
'*God saw that the wickedness of man was great in the earth and that every imagination of the thoughts of his heart was only evil continually…*
And the Lord said I will destroy man whom I have created.'
God has wrought his revenge upon those nuns.

He has destroyed their house and cast their sinful bodies
across the water.
They will never again disobey the Magisterium.

He pauses so all can take this in.

(*Then gently.*) But the child is still lost, drowned in the flood.

MRS COULTER. With respect, sir, *not* drowned, *not* dead.

WHARTON. It swam?

MRS COULTER. She was rescued by a boy.

WHARTON. Where is this boy now?

MRS COULTER. At the mercy of the flood, sir.
    If you would graciously continue to assist me…
    I will make good on my sacred promise and bring her to you.
    A fast river craft would expedite matters, sir…

WHARTON. Give her what she wants.

Various SUITS *go to obey.*

MRS COULTER (*beat*). What will you do with my child?
    When I give her to you?

WHARTON. We will do what we always do when our Church
    is threatened by the forces of darkness…
    We will obey the Bible, Mrs Coulter.

    MRS COULTER *exits.*

3. A Pharmacy

The canoe is now floating through the streets of Oxford.
Morning.

LOUDHAILERS. Owing to severe flooding,
    His Majesty's Government has declared a national emergency.
    Special Measures are now in place.
    All Displaced Citizens must register at the nearest
    emergency station.
    All citizens without ID will be arrested.

    LYRA *has woken up and is screaming.* ALICE *and*
    MALCOLM *at the end of their tether.*

ALICE. NOW YOU'VE WOKEN LYRA WITH YOUR
    STUPID SHOUTING AND BLAMING!

MALCOLM. *YOU* WOKE HER WITH YOUR STUPID
    SHOUTING AND BLAMING!
    Why don't you just go to sleep?

ALICE. BECAUSE I'M FREEZING AND STARVING AND
    SO IS LYRA!

    Sounds of storm and water surges. It frightens them.

MALCOLM (*whispers*). Stop shouting! We're in Oxford! We
    got no ID!
    And it'll be full of people! Coulter and CCD could be
    anywhere!

ALICE (*whispers*). We need to change her and feed her.

MALCOLM (*whispers*). I'm *trying* to get us to firm ground.

    A neon-green pharmacy cross sign somewhere as…

ALICE (*whispers*). Look! It's a pharmacy!
    Stop here! We can get in through the upstairs window!
    We can get powdered milk. And a bottle.
    And some of them nappies you throw away.
    There might be some food for us too.
    (*Picks up* LYRA.) Here we go, Lyra!
    (*And climbs into the pharmacy.*) Brilliant!
    (*There are piles of boxes.*)

They put all their stores up here out of the water!
Tie that thing up and come and forage.
(*Sniffs* LYRA*'s nappy.*) Pheuwgh! That's a champion stink
that is, Lyra!
Let's get you cleaned up, girl!
Now, nappies… talcum powder… and some nice cream for
your sore bum.

*She sources stuff from behind the boxes, and, as she finds
nappies, talcum powder, soothing cream, changes* LYRA…
MALCOLM, *mooring* La Belle Sauvage, *finds something
pinned in the lip of the canoe.*

MALCOLM. Look at this!

ASTA. What is it?

MALCOLM. Card. Under the bulkhead.
(*Reads the card as they climb into the pharmacy.*)
'Lord Asriel, October House, Greenwich, London.'
(*He turns the card over.*)
Message on the other side.
(*Reads.*) 'Malcolm Polstead, your canoe returned.
I gave her to the best boatbuilder in England.
She is now the slippiest vessel on the Thames.
With many thanks. If you need my help at any time be sure
to ask.
Asriel.'

ASTA. Interesting. What are we thinking?

MALCOLM. We need to get Lyra somewhere safe.

ASTA. We've been thinking about that scholastic sanctuary
thing Sister Fenella told us about.

MALCOLM. The current's against us. We'll never get back to
Jordan College.

ASTA. So instead…

MALCOLM. Get plenty of baby supplies here, then go all the
way down the Thames.
Take Lyra to Lord Asriel!

ASTA. Alice won't like it.

MALCOLM. We won't tell her.

ASTA. Why not?

MALCOLM. She can't be trusted. She might give Lyra to *him*.

ASTA. With the hyena dæmon…

MALCOLM. If he's still alive…

ASTA. We both *know* he's still alive.

They both look around. It is a frightening thought.

Shhh!

ALICE *returns with* LYRA *in a new white nappy and holding a big pot of baby-bottom cream. She catches* MALCOLM *unawares, with the message in his hand.*

ALICE. No food except for baby biscuits. But there's nappies and dried milk… what's that?

MALCOLM. Nothing.

ALICE. So what's our plan, *Captain*?

MALCOLM. Go downriver a bit, see if we can turn into a tributary, and circle back home…

ALICE *and* BEN *look at each other, both their noses take in the air.*

ALICE (*to* BEN). Smell that?

BEN. Something's *off*… you know what I mean?

ALICE. I know what you mean.
And for *once* it's not *Lyra*…

MALCOLM. Come on! Stores! Help pack the boat!
(*Starts to pack the boat, throwing stores in.*)
What?

ALICE. Thass a lot of stores just to turn round to get home…

MALCOLM. So?

ALICE. We *are* heading back to The Trout, right?

MALCOLM. Right?

ALICE. No we *ain't*! I can read you like a book, you little
bastard!
(*Grabs him, searches his pockets, finds* ASRIEL's *card*.)
I seen you looking at this. *Greenwich?* We're going to
London?

Flings it to the floor. He goes down for it. She kicks him.

MALCOLM. Ow!

ALICE. You don't *tell* me, you just *expect* me to go, to look
after the kid.
Then you lie about it, you little swine!
I hate liars.
You'*re worse* than Gerard Bonneville!

*She kicks him again and again. He gets hold of a box of
nappies to ward her off but he's no match for her.*

Ooo. What you gonna do with that box of nappies,
Professor?
Hit me over the head? You and whose army?
I'll lay yer out! I'll break your bloody arm! See if you can
paddle *then*!
(*Picks up* LYRA, *very calm and sweet*.) Don't cry!
Alice just lost her temper with a little piece of sewage,
not with *you*, my lovely!
(*Back to* –) Put the bloody box in the bloody canoe, you /
scumbag…

VOICE (*off*). Hey! What you doing in there?

They freeze. Dinghy carrying two OFFICIAL-LOOKING
MEN *a little upstream.*

ALICE (*shows them* LYRA). We got a baby to look after. It's
my sister.

MAN. What you putting in that canoe?

MALCOLM. Blankets and stuff in case we got to be in the boat
another night.

MAN. Why don't you stay in there?

ALICE. What's it got to do with / *you*?

MALCOLM. *Sandra*... this gentleman is just looking after
the place.
We live in *Botley*. We gotta get back.

MAN. What's your name?

MALCOLM. *Richard Parsons*. This is my sister *Sandra*. And
the baby's...

MALCOLM *and* ALICE. *Ellie*.

MALCOLM. We live with our grand/ma.

ALICE. She's bedrid. This is why we gotta get back quick /
sticks.

MAN. You know that's looting?

ALICE. It ent looting, it's borrowing.

MALCOLM. We're only borrowing what we need to stay alive.

ALICE. And keep our little baby sister / alive!

MALCOLM. Soon as the flood goes down our uncle'll come
pay for what we took.

ALICE. We're an honest family.

MALCOLM. Ask anybody in Botley.

MAN. There's an emergency station at the Town Hall in
St Aldate's. Go show your IDs and get registered.

MALCOLM. We'll do that. Thank you very much.

Dinghy rows off.

Get in the canoe. We need to get out of here.
(*Beat.*)
What?

ALICE (*gets in the canoe as with utter disgust and disbelief*).
'Sandra'?

MALCOLM, *red-eared, pushes off. The current takes them,
as...*

4. Emergency Meeting

Back in HANNAH*'s room.* HANNAH *and* NUGENT, *now in dry clothes.*

NUGENT. Dr Relf… if you can go any quicker…

HANNAH (*consulting books as she reads the alethiometer*).
I'm asking if the baby survived the flood.

NUGENT. It must have… they had a canoe, which is more than we had, and *we* survived.

HANNAH. But not the nuns. Those poor, brave nuns.

PAPADIMITRIOU, DR ADNAN, YASMIN AL KHASY, CLUNY – *the opposition at Oakley Street, all academics – arrive in a hurry.*

NUGENT. What have you got?

PAPADIMITRIOU. Geneva are throwing Holy Scripture at everything.

YASMIN. They can detain *persons of suspicion* for as long as they like.

ADNAN. Including anyone involved in research into *Dust*.

NUGENT. Which confirms our intelligence that whatever is emerging in that field
is not to their advantage. What else?

CLUNY. There's someone from the Magisterium pulling strings in Downing Street.
Marisa Coulter was taken in, then released.

PAPADIMITRIOU. With some nice leaving gifts.

CLUNY. High-speed motorboat. Armed escort.

NUGENT. So the baby still holds their interest.
Can't we go faster, Dr Relf?

HANNAH. Alethiometry requires precision and patience.

Beat.

NUGENT. This baby… and *Dust*…

PAPADIMITRIOU. *Both* attracting enormous interest at the same time from the Magisterium.

NUGENT. Are they more connected than we thought?

HANNAH. Affirmation. The baby's still alive.

NUGENT. If the child's still alive we need to get out on the river and find it before Marisa Coulter and the CCD.

They rush off.

5. Dry Land

MALCOLM, ALICE *and* LYRA *in the canoe. Sound of a fast motorboat. Afternoon.*

ALICE. Patrol Boat!

MALCOLM. Get Down!

MRS COULTER (*over a loudhailer*). Attention, All Concerned Citizens. You are required under emergency powers to report all unaccompanied children on river craft.

MALCOLM. Coulter!

COULTER (*loudhailer*). This is for their own safety.

They both duck down. Motorboat roars off.
MALCOLM paddles. ALICE rocks LYRA. Somewhere nearby... a HYENA laugh.

MALCOLM. What was that?

ALICE. Nothing.

MALCOLM. Sounded like a hyena...

ALICE. Didn't! Shut up.
(*Beat.*)
It's just your big stupid imagination, Professor. Okay?

MALCOLM. Okay.

In the middle distance, a Georgian house with gardens sloping down to the flood.

ALICE. Look… a house. A nice warm big house!
There might be some kind people in it who'll give us
some food!

A MAN *swaying in the wind outside the house.*

Yes! There's *a man.*

MALCOLM. It's not… (*i.e. Bonneville?*)

ALICE. It's a *stranger.*

MALCOLM. Go ask if he's got somewhere we can stay.

ALICE. Why *me*?

MALCOLM. He's a *man*. He'll take more notice of you.

ALICE. Got you.
(*She gets out of the canoe, approaches the* MAN.)
Lovely house, darling…

The MAN *teeters. He is absolutely paralytic.*

DRUNK. It ent yours, *darling…*

ALICE. Is it yours?

DRUNK. Tis now.

ALICE. Did you fight for it?

DRUNK. What's it to you?

ALICE. If you *fought* for it belongs to you, no doubt about /
it…

DRUNK. *No doubt about it.* I *fought* for it!
(*He does some drunken sparring, and falls over.*)

ALICE (*whispers to* MALCOLM). E's paralytic. / *You* handle
drunks in the pub. *Your* turn.

MALCOLM. Okay. Take Lyra into the house.

MALCOLM *helps the* DRUNK *up as* ALICE *goes into the
house.*

Sir… you should put up a notice…
'Keep out. Trespassers will be prosecuted.'

DRUNK. I *should*! Get me a hammer…

MALCOLM. I *will*, sir… (*Confidential.*) Sir… there's bad
    people after our baby.

DRUNK. Bastards!

MALCOLM. They might come to your house!

DRUNK. *S'my* house the *bad bastards*!

MALCOLM. You should defend it then!

DRUNK. I should! I will! I got a shotgun!
    (*He has. He waves it around.*)
    Get inside my house. Leave the trespassing bastards to me.

MALCOLM. Don't let them in your house.

DRUNK. No! S'my house!

MALCOLM. Careful. These bastards can be *dangerous*!

DRUNK. *I'm* dangerous!
    (*And swings his shotgun wildly to prove he is.*)

6. Lord Murderer's House

*The kitchen of the Georgian riverside house. There's stew in
a pot on the table, which is laid for one.*

ALICE (*with a screaming, crying* LYRA *in her arms*).
    Lyra… look at the nice warm dry house! Aren't we posh?
    Won't we be a couple of ladies staying here?
    We won't go to London in a freezing canoe, will we?

MALCOLM *enters.*

We'll stay here,
where it's warm and dry and we got a guard outside, guarding.
You'll have a nice warm bottle of milk,
and I'll have this nice stew, then we'll go back to Godstow!

A gunshot. Both freeze.

What's that?

MALCOLM. Probably nothing.
(*Beat.*)
Probably that drunk bastard's shot his own foot off.
(*Beat.*)
I'll go check.
(*Exits.*)

ALICE (*cuddles* LYRA *for comfort*). It's just another stupid
drunk. We're used to *them*, aren't we?
Let's go see if we can find us both some nice warm blankets!

And exits as MALCOLM *runs in.*

MALCOLM. Alice! Alice! Where are you? We got to get out of
here…
The drunk man's *dead*! *Where are you? Where are you?*

Behind him…
BONNEVILLE *emerges from the darkness with his rucksack
and the drunk's shotgun,*
sees MALCOLM, *carefully puts down the rucksack, then…*

BONNEVILLE. Well, well. The pot boy!

The HYENA *goes and sniffs the stew.*

Stew smells *amazing*!

HYENA *laps the stew.*
MALCOLM *stares, terrified.*
Beat.

You know whose house this once was, don't you?

MALCOLM. I don't care whose / house…

BONNEVILLE. This was the infamous Lord Murdstone's house.
He used to bring children here.
Do you know who Lord Murdstone was, pot boy?

MALCOLM. No.

BONNEVILLE. He was also known as Lord Murderer.
He brought children here because this house stands all
on its own,
no neighbours for miles.
He could do what he liked with them here. No one to stop him.
What do you think he did with them, pot boy?

MALCOLM. I don't care what he did, I don't / want to hear this...

BONNEVILLE. He took them apart, bit by bit... while they were still alive.
That was his special pleasure.
While they were still alive, pot boy. Can you imagine?

MALCOLM. I don't want to.

BONNEVILLE. And yet you *are* imagining, aren't you?

MALCOLM *clearly is.*

Can't you *feel* that this is a wicked place?

He lets MALCOLM *imagination work.*

Can't you smell the thick dried blood in the walls...?
And the air, full of ghosts.
Can you see them?

MALCOLM. See who?

BONNEVILLE. The spirits of the air and the earth...
Once you learn to see them, you realise the world is thronged with them...
Look! One behind you!

MALCOLM *whips round.*

MALCOLM. There's nothing there!

BONNEVILLE. Oh, but there *is*! *Breathe in,* pot boy...

MALCOLM *eventually, takes a breath.*

No clean wind, am I right?
That's because this air entering your chest was last in the lungs of tortured children...

He lets this settle into MALCOLM*'s brain.*

Makes you wonder what else is out there that you can't see, doesn't it?
Listen... you'll hear their desperate little whispers...

He lets MALCOLM *listen.*

and then you'll begin to see them like *I* see them.

MALCOLM *goes for the shotgun, tries to wrest it from*
BONNEVILLE. *Impasse.*

You're stronger than you look, pot boy.

MALCOLM. *Malcolm Polstead.*

BONNEVILLE. Malcolm *Polstead.* You seem like a clever boy,
Malcolm.
You should be around clever people, don't you think?

MALCOLM. I'm alright thank you.

BONNEVILLE. We're not men of violence, Malcolm. We're
men of imagination.
Let's stand down and talk like scholars.

ALICE *returns with a sleeping* LYRA, *stands very still.*
MALCOLM *sees* ALICE. BONNEVILLE *doesn't.*

MALCOLM. Okay. Tell me about *Dust.*
Do you think Rusakov has got it right?

BONNEVILLE. Rusakov has got it right as far as he goes, but
I get it right and I go much further…
A prison cell proved the perfect place for concentrated
thought, Malcolm.
This rucksack contains all the work I did there.

MALCOLM. Work about Dust?

BONNEVILLE. How do you know about Dust?

MALCOLM. I don't. Tell me what it is.

BONNEVILLE. It's a name for what happens when matter
begins to understand itself.

MALCOLM. Like… it's *conscious*?

BONNEVILLE. Exactly. Conscious beings like you and I make
Dust all the time.

MALCOLM. By thinking?

BONNEVILLE. And feeling and reflecting and passing it on…
My papers contain ideas that will blow your mind…
I have the strongest hunch that somewhere

very close
are windows into *infinite* other worlds…

MALCOLM. That's just in dreams.

BONNEVILLE. Not *just* in dreams, Malcolm…

ALICE *stealthily picks up the knife.*

'If the doors of perception were cleansed,
then everything would appear to man as it is – infinite.'
Put down the knife, Alice. And give me the baby.

MALCOLM. Why do you want her?

ALICE. Cos he's a bloody pervert!

BONNEVILLE. She's my daughter, Malcolm.

ALICE. No she's not!

BONNEVILLE. Are you *sure* about that, Alice? Have you *met*
Marisa Coulter, Malcolm?
Any man would be *thrilled* to make a baby with her.

MALCOLM. Lord Asriel's her father!

BONNEVILLE. Alright then… I'm going to roast her and eat
her, I bet she tastes delic/ious…

ALICE *spits at him.* MALCOLM *grabs a kitchen knife.*

MALCOLM. Sorry but…

He sticks a kitchen knife in BONNEVILLE*'s thigh.*
BONNEVILLE *screams and lets go the gun. He tries,*
in agony to pull out the knife.

Sorry!

BONNEVILLE *grabs* MALCOLM*'s foot.*

BONNEVILLE. Oh no, *you're* staying with *me!*

MALCOLM. Alice! Take Lyra and run!

But ALICE *instead grabs the gun and points it at*
BONNEVILLE.

ALICE. Let him go!

BONNEVILLE. You wouldn't shoot me, would you, Alice?

ALICE *wavers*.

You really like me too much, don't you, Alice?

She turns the gun on the HYENA *and shoots it in the leg.*
HYENA *screams with agony, tries to stand but falls on a leg that is barely there.*
BONNEVILLE *screams at the same time and lets go of* MALCOLM's *foot.*

ALICE. *Run*, Malcolm! Run!

ALICE *drops the gun, picks up* LYRA, *snatches* BONNEVILLE's *rucksack, runs.*

MALCOLM. 'We're not men of violence – (*He is about to stab* BONNEVILLE *again. Instead –*) we're men of imagination.' (*Seizes the rucksack.*) I'm taking this! Imagine that! (*And runs.*)

7. Canoe

They are in the canoe. MALCOLM's *teeth are chattering alarmingly. Dusk.*

MALCOLM. My teeth won't stop chattering!

ALICE. It's *shock*, Malcolm.
You probably need a little cry…

MALCOLM. I'm just *cold* okay? (*He's not.*)

ALICE. Okay.

MALCOLM. Okay. (*But he starts shaking with trying to stop his teeth chattering.*)

ALICE. If you want a little cry, I won't tell on you.

LYRA *starts crying.*

Look! Lyra's crying…

MALCOLM. I'm *not* crying.
  (*Beat.*)
  Did we kill him?

  Silence until...

ALICE. Probably.
  (*Beat.*)
  I hope so.

MALCOLM. He was bleeding *a lot.*
  (*Beat.*)
  I think there's an artery there in his leg.
  And that dæmon...

ALICE. I shot her. (*She allows the thought in.*)
  He can't live if I've shot *her* surely. (*It's a dreadful,
  terrifying thought.*)

MALCOLM. No.

ALICE. Anyway, they won't be able to move. Neither of them.

MALCOLM. Hope so.
  (*Beat. The thought builds.*)
  Every time I try to do something safe for Lyra,
  I just make it more dangerous for her!
  I just murdered somebody!

  And bursts into tears. LYRA *cries too. Then...*

ALICE. So did I!

  ALICE *cries too.*

MALCOLM. Sorry!

  They cry it out separately until...

ALICE. Alright. Stop. Enough crying! What's done is done!
  We got a baby to look after!
  (*Beat.*)
  Mal.

MALCOLM. What?

ALICE. You done good.
  (*Silence for a bit until...*)

MALCOLM. I'm *so starving*!

ALICE. Me too!

This makes them cry-laugh.

I'm gonna open that that hyena bastard's rucksack… see if there's something to eat.

MALCOLM. I could *kill* for a biscuit!

ALICE. S'not funny!
What the bleeding hell is this?

She's found a small box. She opens it. An alethiometer.
MALCOLM *takes it.*

MALCOLM. It's an alethiometer!
Dr Relf says there's only six of these in the whole world!
He shouldn't have one… he must have stolen it.

ALICE. I wish he'd stolen some *food*!

MALCOLM (*he's examining it as closely as he did the acorn*).
I wonder if you can get inside it somehow… see how it works.

ALICE. There's just that thing…

MALCOLM. Alethio/meter…

ALICE. And loads of bloody papers –
(*Reads.*) 'An analysis of some philosophical implications of the Rusakov field
by Gerard Bonneville, PhD.' It's full of equations and signs… here, Professor, you can probably understand it.
(*She hands them to* MALCOLM.)

MALCOLM. I doubt it! (*Scans the papers.*) Must be his research…
(*Reads.*) 'We conscious beings make Dust.
We renew it all the time, by thinking, by reflecting, by gaining wisdom and passing it on.'
We should take this to a college or something… we better keep it dry.

Searchlights strafe the area.

CCD. This is the CCD.

ALICE. Oh bloody hell! CCD!

CCD. You are Unidentifiable River Craft.
  We need to investigate. You are advised to hold your position.

MALCOLM. We're sitting ducks out here!

CCD. This is CCD. Maintain your position.
  Repeat. Maintain your position.

  They get the into the bank, take LYRA, *and start running,
  trying to dodge the searchlights.*

  Do not disembark from your vessel.
  Repeat. Do not disembark from your vessel.

  *Suddenly they are fallen upon by a terrifying group who pull
  them into the trees as searchlights strafe.*

GEORGE BOATWRIGHT (*whispers to his followers*). Quick!
  Hide their boat!

  They cover the canoe.

8. Refugee Camp

A makeshift camp under the cover of thick woodland.

MALCOLM. Mr Boatwright?

GEORGE BOATWRIGHT. Yes. Keep quiet and still!

  All keep very still, very quiet, as… searchlights strafe.

CCD. Where've they gone?
  Where've they gone?
  Light the bank!

  Searchlights crawl from left to right.

  Are they hiding in the trees? Light the trees!

  *Searchlights strafe a bit higher…
  Everybody keeps very quiet and still.*

Anything?
Nothing. They must have slipped through somehow! Try
downstream!

Patrol-boat engine fires… .
everybody quiet and still until… sound of patrol boats dies
away.

GEORGE BOATWRIGHT. Won't be back tonight.

Everyone starts fettling for food, drink, warmth and sleep.

You must be worn out. Tea, then food then sleep. You
remember my Charlie…

CHARLIE. Hello, Malcolm.
(*To everybody.*) Everybody… this is Malcolm! From
The Trout!
Brenda Polstead's lad!

Everybody signals hello.

GEORGE BOATWRIGHT. Get him some tea! You want some
tea, Malcolm?

CHARLIE. This is Alice Parslow!
Alice Parslow! Pot girl from The Trout! George's second
home!

Everybody signals hello.

You look like you need some tea, girl.
(*Sees* LYRA.) Who's this? He? She?

MALCOLM. She. Lyra.

CHARLIE. Phyeugh! She needs a clean nappy. You got food
for her?

ALICE. Milk powder in the boat.

    CHARLIE, LYRA *and* ALICE *go towards the boat.*

MALCOLM. Where are we?

GEORGE BOATWRIGHT. Chilterns. Safe for the time being.
These other folk all like us,
in the same position kind of thing…

MALCOLM. Hiding from the authorities?

GEORGE BOATWRIGHT. Hiding from the authorities kind of thing, yes.
But you don't enquire too close, Malcolm, it ent polite.

ANDREW (*coming forward*). Hi, Malcolm.

MALCOLM. Andrew –

ALICE *returns with* LYRA.

ANDREW. This is a bit different from *school*, isn't it!

MALCOLM. Yes.

ANDREW. That your sister?

MALCOLM. No!

ANDREW. I mean that baby.

MALCOLM. Lyra.

ANDREW. Funny name.

MALCOLM. Yeah well. We're just looking after her during the flood. You here with your parents?

ANDREW. Just my auntie Doris.

DORIS. Doris Whicher. Fugitive! Welcome to the great outdoors.
(DORIS *is quite drunk. With an almost-empty bottle*.)
Ask George and Charlie for sommat from their liquor stash…
it's too bloody cold to get to sleep without it!

MALCOLM. Did you get flooded out?

ANDREW. Yeah. Lots of people in our street got drowned.

MALCOLM. Your mum and dad?

ANDREW. Yeah.

DORIS. Worst flood since Noah. 'Forty days and forty nights.'

MALCOLM. Sorry.

ANDREW. What's that baby's name?

MALCOLM. I said. Lyra.

ANDREW. Funny name.

MALCOLM. Yeah you said.

CHARLIE. Alice, this milk warm enough?

MALCOLM. Who is everyone?

GEORGE BOATWRIGHT. There's my sister Susan and her wife Emerald. The others are… just others.

ANDREW, *unseen by everyone else, exits*.

So what'd everybody in The Trout say after I ran?

MALCOLM. They said you were the only person ever escaped from the CCD.

GEORGE BOATWRIGHT. Yeah?

MALCOLM. It's all got worse since you disappeared. Being *good* doesn't seem to matter any more.
It seems to be better to do a *bad thing*. Because doing a *bad* thing might do some good!

GEORGE BOATWRIGHT. You just had to do something bad, Malcolm?

MALCOLM. Yes.

GEORGE BOATWRIGHT. Want to tell me what?

MALCOLM. No. I can't. Cos someone else is implicated so I can't [*tell you*]…

MALCOLM *starts shaking*. GEORGE *puts his hand on* MALCOLM's *shoulder*.

GEORGE BOATWRIGHT. You probably come up against something evil you had to deal with…?

MALCOLM, *after a bit, nods*.

When you come up against evil, you learn quick enough it's got a *certainty*
and so it'll do *anything*, right?

MALCOLM. Right.

GEORGE BOATWRIGHT. Evil ent got nothing to stop it doing
      what it wants,
      while good has one hand tied behind his bloody back, right?

MALCOLM. Yes.

GEORGE BOATWRIGHT. Sometimes good has to just untie
      that hand and strike with it.
      That's the times we live in now.

MALCOLM. Right.

GEORGE BOATWRIGHT. Whatever anybody here done, boy,
      they probably ad to do.
      (*Beat*.)
      Just like you probably had to. Right…?

MALCOLM. Right.

GEORGE BOATWRIGHT. Then stop dwelling on it.

CHARLIE. Here. Some stew, Malcolm. Almost as good as your
      mum's…

This gives MALCOLM *a wobble.*

What?

GEORGE BOATWRIGHT. His mum, Charlie.
      She's alright, boy. The Trout survived. Cellar flooded,
      but Brenda says she's turning it into an indoor swimming pool.
      We'll get you back to her when it's safe.

Lights appear.

Hello… will-o'-the-wisp time… so we can see what we're
      eating!
      Secret Commonwealth's on our side, see?
      Even this flood's on our side, giving us more getaways,
      shallow and deep.
      Water's on our side, not theirs.

MALCOLM. How come?

GEORGE BOATWRIGHT. The creatures in the water. I don't
      mean fish and voles.
      I mean the old gods. Old Father Thames. Seen him a few
      times, with his crown and weeds and his trident. He's on
      our side.

Tom Simms saw a mermaid near Henley. Sea was so full she
came right upriver.
Tom Simms swore if he saw her again, he'd go off with her.
Two days later he disappeared... I reckon he done just that.

CHARLIE. I reckon if it was Tom Simms, he was drunk and
that was a porpoise.

DORIS. I thought I saw a little merman once but it was an otter.

GEORGE BOATWRIGHT. Weren't a porpoise, weren't an otter.
He spoke to her, she spoke back. Had a voice sweeter than
a chime of bells.
Ten to one he's living with her now out in the German Ocean.

CHARLIE (*collecting plates*). He'll be bloody cold if he is.
Shut yer yap now.
These kids are exhausted. Help me put em to bed.

GEORGE BOATWRIGHT (*blankets, sleeping bags, etc*.).
You three can stay here with us long as you need to.
You're safe as houses here.
(*To* DORIS.) Weren't an otter.

Everybody hunkers down to sleep, DORIS *in a drunken
slump nearby.*
ALICE, LYRA *and finally* MALCOLM *tucked in as one of
the* REFUGEES *sings to a guitar.*
The song helps everybody sleep, except MALCOLM *and*
ALICE, LYRA *between them.*

ALICE. I can't sleep!

They lie staring.

If I close my eyes I see *him*.

MALCOLM. If I close my eyes, there's hurt animals all torn up
and they're bleeding.
(*Beat*.)
We're murderers, Alice.

ALICE. Mal, you got to stop *thinking*.

MALCOLM. We both got to stop thinking.

ALICE. Be like Lyra. She's thinking even though she doesn't
have words.

MALCOLM. I know. I'm *trying*.

ALICE. You need some *sleep*.

MALCOLM. *I know.*

ALICE. Close your eyes.

> *She watches him close his eyes. Satisfied, she closes her eyes.*
>
> We're safe as houses.
>
> *Both lie until* MALCOLM *'s eyes open. Sits bolt upright.*
>
> What? *What?*

MALCOLM. Where's Andrew? I don't see him.

ALICE. Perhaps he sleeps somewhere else…

> MALCOLM *shakes* DORIS *awake.*

DORIS. What?

MALCOLM. Andrew's not here! Where is he?

DORIS. Snuck off again, has he? Is he off doing that bloody League / nonsense again?

MALCOLM. The League of St Alexander?

DORIS. That's the one.

MALCOLM. He *hates* the League.

DORIS. No… he's one of their like secret prefects.
But don't tell the Boatwrights or they'll kick / him out…

MALCOLM (*to* ALICE). We got to go. Right now. Get Lyra!

> *But it's too late.*
> ANDREW, *a severe* CHILD PROTECTON OFFICER *and* TWO ARMED POLICE *enter.*
>
> Mr Boatwright!
>
> GEORGE BOATWRIGHT *and the rest of the camp wake up, leap up, but it's too late.*
> *The* ARMED POLICE *train guns on the* REFUGEES *as…*

ARMED POLICE 1. Alright, everybody. Nobody gets hurt if everybody keeps nice and calm.

CHILD PROTECTION OFFICER. Where's this baby? Don't make us wait.

ANDREW. There she is! *Knew* she wasn't your sister! (*He flips his lapel. A League of St Alexander badge.*) I knew you were at the devil's work!

CHILD PROTECTION OFFICER. Take the baby.

ARMED POLICE go for LYRA. GEORGE BOATWRIGHT *goes for them.*
One of them hits him with his gun. GEORGE BOATWRIGHT *drops.*

CHARLIE. You bastard!

DORIS. See what you done, Andrew Whicher?

One of the ARMED POLICE *keeps the rest of the camp at bay with his pointed gun.*
The other takes the baby from a biting and spitting and clawing ALICE.

ALICE. No. *No!* She's *mine*!

But he's too strong for her.

MALCOLM. She's *ours*!

MALCOLM *piles in but receives a shocking blow to the head. The* POLICE *give* LYRA *to the* CHILD PROTECTION OFFICER. *Both have their guns trained on the camp members.*

ARMED POLICE 1. Nobody gets hurt if everybody minds their own business and leaves us to do ours!

The three, with LYRA, *back off and exit.* CHARLIE *goes to* GEORGE BOATWRIGHT. MALCOLM *tries to rise.*

MALCOLM. World's spinning!

ASTA. It's the blow on the head.

DORIS (*to* ANDREW). See what you done now, you daft little bastard?

CHARLIE. George, George darling… you alright?

GEORGE BOATWRIGHT. I'm alright. (*He stands*.) Start
  packing up. Ent safe here any more.
  We been found. We got to move on!

  The REFUGEES *frantically collect their belongings.*

ASTA. You can't stand up yet. Keep still!

  But MALCOLM *struggles to his feet, heads for* ANDREW,
  who puts his hands up in defence. MALCOLM *knocks them
  aside, hits* ANDREW *hard in the face.*

MALCOLM. Who were those men? Where have they gone?

ANDREW. To give that baby you stole *back*!

  MALCOLM *hits him hard in the face.*

MALCOLM. Where are they taking Lyra?

ANDREW. You broke my jaw!

  Then ALICE *is there slapping and scratching* ANDREW.

  No, don't hit me!

ALICE. Tell us who they were!

ANDREW. I dunno.

GEORGE BOATWRIGHT. Tell the truth, Andrew, or we leave
  you and your auntie to fend for yourselves.

MALCOLM. Where did you go to find them?

ANDREW. Wallingford! The Sisters of Holy Obedience!
  The League of St Alexander says you should tell about
  suspicious stuff.
  I bet you *stole* that baby. I bet you're *sinners*!

  MALCOLM *tries to throttle* ANDREW.

MALCOLM. How far is this place? How far? HOW FAR?

DORIS. George... *stop him*!

GEORGE BOATWRIGHT. Andrew's got to decide which side
  he's on, Doris...

ALICE. Mal... e can't tell if e can't breathe.
(*Gently eases* MALCOLM's *throttling hands...*
To ANDREW.) I won't let him kill yer if you just tell us how
to get there...

ANDREW (*wincing and bleeding*). Ent far. A mile downstream.
It's the highest place. With a spire.

GEORGE BOATWRIGHT. You got your information,
Malcolm. You better look sharp.

MALCOLM *and* ALICE *collect the rucksack, and get in the
canoe into the flood again.*

MALCOLM. Thank you, Mr Boatwright. And s*orry*!

As they paddle off, GEORGE BOATWRIGHT *picks up*
ANDREW *by the scruff of his neck, hurls him at* DORIS.

GEORGE BOATWRIGHT. Get him packed up, then follow the
others, Doris.
We got to find somewhere new where we can all make
ourselves invisible again!

DORIS *drags* ANDREW *off.* GEORGE BOATWRIGHT
picks up his small rucksack and exits.

9. Mal

On the flood again. Night. Out of the mist looms the Priory of the Sisters of Holy Obedience, forbidding and sinister.

ALICE. Building with a spire.

MALCOLM. This is it.

ALICE. It's like a bloody fortress.

MALCOLM. I'll tie her up. You stay with the canoe.

ALICE. Why?

MALCOLM. Because she's an Albion oak-bark and I don't want to lose her again.
Also, one person is less noticeable than two.

ALICE. Well, *be careful*, Mal… .

MALCOLM. You keep calling me 'Mal'.

ALICE. So? Malcolm's a horrible name. Mal suits you better.

A moment between them.

MALCOLM. Right.

Very mutually embarrassing.

10. The Priory of the Sisters of Holy Obedience

THE SISTERS OF HOLY OBEDIENCE *arrive out of the darkness, chanting.*
Behind them, cot after cot after cot of sleeping children.

MALCOLM (*to* ASTA). It's the nursery.

ASTA. Shhh!

They creep round the perimeter, into the corridors, but…

SISTER MARIA THERESE. Boy! Stand still!

ASTA. Act dumb!

SISTER MARIA THERESE. What are you doing out of your bed?

MALCOLM. Going to the lavatory, sister.

SISTER MARIA THERESE. Next door to the nursery? After sunset?
Children are to stay in their beds until dawn.

MALCOLM. I wet my bed, sister. Then I got lost.

SISTER MARIA THERESE (*delivers a resounding slap on the side of his head*). Filthy brat.
Go to the bathroom and wash yourself.
Then take an oilcloth and fresh blanket from the airing cupboard and go back to bed.
We'll discuss your punishment in the morning.

MALCOLM. Sorry, sister.

SISTER MARIA THERESE. Stop whining! Do as I tell you and *no talking*.

MALCOLM. Yes, sister.

SISTER MARIA THERESE *glides away*. MALCOLM *doubles back into…*

The nursery! Lyra should be here!

They survey the quietly sleeping babies.

ASTA. There's *millions* of them.

MALCOLM. Don't exaggerate… will we recognise her?

ASTA. Let's see.

They go down the row…forensic look at each baby.

MALCOLM. Too small.

ASTA (*next one*). The head's too round.

MALCOLM (*next one*). Too fair.

ASTA (*next one*). Too big.

MALCOLM (*next one*). That's an *amazing* amount of black hair on a baby!

SISTER PAULINA. Follow me, please.

ASTA. Someone coming! *Hide!*

> MALCOLM *hides under one of the cots.*
> SISTER PAULINA, *with clipboard, arrives with*
> MRS COULTER.

SISTER PAULINA. Taking a child during the night. It's really not correct procedure, Mrs Coulter.

MRS COULTER. It's a matter of urgency, sister.
(*She hands her a letter of authorisation.*)
My daughter was admitted in the early hours of this /
morning...

SISTER PAULINA. Your *daughter*? (*Consults papers.*)
But this was a Security of the Holy Spirit admiss/ion...

MRS COULTER. Of course it was. The Security of the Holy Spirit report to *me*.

SISTER PAULINA. I wasn't told.

MRS COULTER. I asked them as a matter of urg/ency...

SISTER PAULINA. It's not down in the accompanying / notes.

MRS COULTER. Nevertheless... Sister...

SISTER PAULINA. Paulina.

MRS COULTER. I really don't want to bring the wrath of the Magisterium down / on you.

SISTER PAULINA. Sisters of Holy Obedience don't care for threats, / Mrs Coulter.

MRS COULTER. What a Sister of Holy Obedience must care about, Sister Paulina, is surely... *obeying*.
The Magisterium has sanctioned me to take my child to safety.
If you do not do as I ask, I will have no choice but to let them know you...
Sister Paulina, is it?... obstructed me.

Battle of wills.

I will take her now. Which one is she?

SISTER PAULINA (*beat*). This one.

MRS COULTER (*taking the baby*). Thank you, Sister Paulina.
I have all I need.

SISTER PAULINA. The Sisters of Holy Obedience are happy if
you're happy.
(*Exits in righteous piety.*)

MRS COULTER *opens the baby's covers a little… the*
GOLDEN MONKEY *goes on its hind legs to look.*
Both stare at LYRA *for a long time.*

MRS COULTER. You. Lyra. You're my baby.
(*Stares even longer.*)
You're the subject of *a* prophecy. I'm Marisa Coulter.
Look at us! How could we have let ourselves get into this
mess?
(*She stares at the baby. Underneath her calm, she's fighting
some other emotion.*
Then, to the GOLDEN MONKEY.) Get down.
We need to go.

They exit.

ASTA. Come on! We need to follow her!
(*Goes as far as she can from her human.*)
Malcolm!

MALCOLM, *however, is transfixed by the cot they hid
behind.* ASTA *comes back.*

What?

MALCOLM. She's taken the wrong baby!
She's taken the wrong baby!
This is Lyra! Lyra!

ASTA. Yes! This is *Pan*.

MALCOLM. I was afraid I wouldn't know you again but I'd
know you among *a million* babies.

They pick up both baby and dæmon.

Come on!

11. People Come Back

Back at the canoe, ALICE *is waiting.* ALICE *and* BEN *are cold and scared and frightened… they try to locate the scary noises all around them…*

ALICE. Ben… you awake?

BEN. Course I'm awake. If *you're* awake, *I'm* awake.

ALICE. I'm scared.
  Are you scared?

BEN. Course I'm scared.
  If *you're* scared… *I'm* scared.

  Something on the river causes water movement. It's scary!

ALICE. I *hate* water!

BEN. Mal's been gone a long time.

ALICE. He'll come back.

BEN. People don't always come back to us
  even if they say they will.

ALICE. I *know* that, Ben.

BEN. I know you know that.

ALICE. Mal will come back.

BEN. Will he?

ALICE. Course he will.

  They wait.
  They both hear the sound of someone approaching!
  Both terrified… then MALCOLM *arrives suddenly*
  with LYRA.

  Took your bloody time, didn't you?

MALCOLM. I got her! I rescued her!
  Right from under Coulter's nose!

ALICE. Coulter?

MALCOLM. Coulter.

ALICE. Here, give her to me.
Gimme your hand!
I got it steady.

She really hasn't but MALCOLM*'s in the canoe.*

You did really well, Mal.

MALCOLM *pushes off. He's elated. The current takes them as* ALICE *greets* LYRA.

Ello, sweetheart!
You slept through all this?
That's because you *knew* Mal wouldn't rest till he rescued you!

MALCOLM *goes pink.*

We *trust* Mal, don't we?

MALCOLM *goes pinker.*

We think Mal's the *cat's pyjamas*, don't we?

MALCOLM *goes puce with pleased embarrassment.*

You're gonna let Alice have a nice sleep too now, aren't you?
(*She yawns and slows.*)
Yes you are…

And falls asleep. MALCOLM *stares at the sleeping* ALICE.

ASTA. What?
What?

MALCOLM (*quoting*). 'The mist clears and you suddenly
understand that girls are actually rather wonderful
and what you want most in the world.'

ASTA. This is *Alice*!

MALCOLM. I know.

ASTA. We *hate* Alice!

MALCOLM. She thinks I'm the cat's pyjamas.

ASTA. Cats don't have pyjamas.

MALCOLM (*to* ALICE, *very soft and tender*). Alice?

She sighs a bit, turns so she is on her back.

Alice?

He kisses her on her lips.
She wakes, at the same time fetching him a good clout
around his ears.
ALICE *may have been disturbed in her sleep like this*
before…

ALICE. Don't You Touch Me!

She's on guard. BEN *is on guard. She realises it is*
MALCOLM *who kissed her.*

MALCOLM. Sorry!

ALICE. What *The Fuck*, Malcolm?

MALCOLM. Sorry!
I just suddenly wanted to / kiss…

ALICE. Well I'm not Sleeping Beauty and for sure you're no
Prince!
Get paddling, Polstead!
Get me to dry land.
I *hate* water.

MALCOLM, *shamefaced and confused, paddles.*
ALICE, *furious, confused and frightened, sits clutching*
LYRA.

12. Death's Dark Kingdom

A HYENA *laugh somewhere startles them.*

ALICE. Was that?

MALCOLM. Can't be.

Then the roar of a motorboat
And searchlights across them…

CCD again!

ALICE. There! Dry land!

MALCOLM. It's a graveyard.

ALICE. It may be a graveyard but it's still dry land.

MALCOLM. It's raining.

ALICE. I know that!

MALCOLM. I feel like something that's died.

ALICE. I wish you *were* something that's died!
Here, you hold Lyra, *I'll* find some firewood…

He tries to follow her.

On my *own*, Prince Charming! Moor up.

MALCOLM *takes* LYRA, ALICE *looks among the*
gravestones.

BEN. You should cut him some slack.

ALICE. Shut up. (*She sees the steps to an underground*
mausoleum.)

BEN (*he is shaking*). There might be some dry wood down
here.

ALICE. Coffin lid or something.

BEN. Gotta do what we gotta do.

ALICE *is about to go down into the crypt when* HANNAH
and the others emerge from behind the gravestones
surrounding it. PAPADIMITRIOU *and* CLUNY *seize*
ALICE.

PAPADIMITRIOU. Stay where you are! Is *this* him?

HANNAH (*shines her torch in* ALICE*'s face*). No.

CLUNY. This isn't a boy with a canoe?

HANNAH. This is *a girl*!

CLUNY. The alethiometer reading was so specific.
      A riverside graveyard. Mausoleum. So! What's gone wrong?

HANNAH (*something lingers on the edge of* HANNAH*'s
      consciousness*). Do I know you?

ALICE. Don't think so.

HANNAH. You seem familiar.

ALICE. I got one of those faces.

HANNAH. What are you doing here?

ALICE. Looking for dry wood for a fire. I thought there might
      be summink down this cellar / thing.

HANNAH. Mausoleum.

ALICE. Big word for a hole in the ground.

HANNAH. It's a place for the dead.

ALICE. I don't think they're gonna mind!

HANNAH. What's your name, please?

ALICE. Sandra.

HANNAH. Sandra. We're looking for a boy. He's looking after
      a baby.

ALICE. Girls look after babies. Boys don't.

HANNAH. This one does. He's in a canoe. And we are very
      concerned for him.
      (*Shines torch in* ALICE*'s face*.)
      Excuse me, are you sure we've never met?

ALICE. *Really* don't think so. I'm Sandra Parsons. From
      London. Now homeless.
      Can you get that out of my face?

PAPADIMITRIOU. The boy's not here. Let's check the map for another riverside cemetery. *Come on.*

CLUNY. Professor Relf, it's not him. Let's…

PAPADIMITRIOU.…leave her to her grave-robbing.

ALICE. I don't think the dead'll mind helping me when I'm just trying to stay alive!

HANNAH. We'll leave you to it / then, Sandra.

ALICE (*on the attack*). Thank you very much, Ladies and Gents!

They are retreating.

Homeless thieving trash here! (*Shouts after their retreating figures.*) Yeah, get back to your nice warm beds! Homeless and Proud of it!

They all exit. She's back with MALCOLM.

MALCOLM. Why are you shouting?

ALICE. There were people here. Not CCD but asking for a boy with a baby.

He picks up the paddle as a weapon.

MALCOLM. Oh shit.

ALICE. Calm down. I got rid of them. Come on, there's a cellar thing back there.
We can keep dry.

And they approach the mausoleum.

MALCOLM (*a bit scared, a bit disapproving*). It's a mausoleum. (*Pronounced like linoleum.*)

ALICE (*correcting him*). *Mausoleum*, thicko.

MALCOLM. Still…

ALICE. It's cover. Get in!

MALCOLM *is about to go down the steps when* BONNEVILLE *emerges.*
He is pale and swaying. He is carrying his HYENA, *who has lost a second leg and is howling and whimpering with pain.*

BONNEVILLE. Malcolm Polstead!
    (*To* HYENA.) Get his daemon!

    HYENA *grabs* ASTA.
    Both ASTA *and* MALCOLM *scream simultaneously.*
    MALCOLM *is rooted to the spot, but struggles.*
    BEN *barks furiously.*

ASTA. Malcolm! Help me!

MALCOLM. I can't move!

    MALCOLM *tries to move but can't.* ASTA *screams in agony
    in the* HYENA*'s bite.*

BONNEVILLE. Struggle all you like, Malcolm Polstead!
    You crippled my dæmon and she wants her revenge!
    You stabbed me in my leg and now *your* legs won't work!
    How does it feel, Malcolm?

    MALCOLM *groans and writhes.*

    You have my alethiometer and my papers, you thieving
    bastards
    and there's *a price* to pay for that.
    I'll take the baby.

ALICE. You fucking won't.

BONNEVILLE. I fucking will.

MALCOLM (*still immobile*). Alice, Run! Take Lyra to London!

    ALICE *tries to run with* LYRA *as* BEN *runs at*
    BONNEVILLE *and tries to bite him.*

BEN. Let Asta go, you bastard!

BONNEVILLE (*he seizes* BEN, *and shakes him violently*). I've
    got your disgusting little mongrel now!
    You're not running *anywhere*, Alice!

    ALICE *is now in pain and immobile.*

    You shot my dæmon so *she* couldn't run
    now *you* can't run either, Alice!
    Put the baby down.

    ALICE *tries to run but can't.*

Down, Alice.

She places LYRA *on the ground.*

Malcolm. Watch this. Lie down, Alice.

ALICE *curls up on the ground.* BONNEVILLE *flings* BEN
aside. BEN *lies curled up on the ground. Both he and*
ALICE *are in too much pain to struggle now.*
BONNEVILLE *starts undoing his trousers.*

I'm going to finally fuck Alice.
(*Discards the knife.*)
Then I think I'll kill her.
Let's see who it hurts most – her or you!

The HYENA *laughs at this, releasing* ASTA.

ASTA. She's let me go!

MALCOLM *can move. He picks up the canoe paddle and,*
still in pain, raises it, strikes. BONNEVILLE *falls to the*
ground.
MALCOLM *straddles him and presses the paddle stem to*
his neck, suffocating him.

BONNEVILLE. Go on then, kill me, you little shit!

MALCOLM *presses even harder. The paddle breaks.*

Peace at last!

BONNEVILLE *falls still.*
The HYENA *vanishes into thin air.*

ALICE (*stands over* BONNEVILLE). *Bastard! Bastard!*

MALCOLM. He can't hear you!
He's dead!
Come on. Run!

13. A Witch

MALCOLM *holding the shattered paddle,* ALICE, *carrying*
LYRA, *into the canoe… canoe into the current.*
MALCOLM *starts to paddle.*
Then, sees his broken paddle is just a stick now…

MALCOLM. This is useless!
   (*Throws it away in disgust.*)
   I'm useless!
   I wish I was home!
   I'm going to sleep!
   (*Wraps himself in his coat and blacks out the world.*)

ALICE. Malcolm?

No answer.

Mal?

No answer.

Prince Charming?
Just us girls, then, Lyra?

She cuddles her very close. Out of the morning mist…
TILDA VASSARA, *a witch, emerges, holding her cloud*
pine, seeming to walk on water.
ALICE *stares,* BEN *quivers all over,* ALICE *rubs her tired*
eyes, focuses.

ALICE. Am I just seeing you because I'm very tired?

TILDA VASSARA. No. We're generally visible. We *can* make
   ourselves invisible…
   But it's quite hard work.
   (*She comes to* ALICE's *side.*)
   I was looking for something.
   (*Touches* LYRA's *cheek.*)
   This. Are you her mother?

ALICE. No. But if you try take her away from me, I'll kill yer.

TILDA VASSARA. No need for that. She is quite safe from me.
   As are you, Brave Girl.

ALICE. You ain't got no dæmon!
   (*This frightens and disconcerts her.*)

TILDA VASSARA. I do have a dæmon. An Arctic tern.
He's in Sweden on an errand for me.
We witches can separate from our dæmons.
And we all have *enormous* curiosity about this little girl!
(*She takes* LYRA*'s hand.*) I just wanted to see her for myself.
Hello *Eve*.

ALICE. No. She's *Lyra*.

TILDA VASSARA. *Lyra*.
Also, Eve the second, mother of all the living, the cause of
all sin.
You're going to cause such a stir, aren't you?
You're going to change the world, aren't you, Eve the second?

LYRA *burbles*.

We will all watch your progress with interest, little girl.
Where are you taking her?

ALICE. Oxford if we can.

TILDA VASSARA. You can't. The water will take you where
you need to go.

ALICE. We broke our paddle.

TILDA VASSARA. I saw. You can manage without it. Trust the
boat.

She stirs up the water. The canoe accelerates dramatically.
TILDA VASSARA *vanishes*.
The speed of the canoe jolts MALCOLM *awake*.

MALCOLM. What? Should I paddle?

ALICE. No. Trust the boat.

*Suddenly the boat is seized by the current and swept off at
great speed.*
*Past Chelsea, Battersea Power Station, the Palace of
Westminster, St Paul's, Tower Bridge... all half-submerged.*
As they reach Greenwich, La Belle Sauvage *finally submits
to the power of the flood and begins to break up.*

14. October House, Greenwich

The terrace of October House, on the Thames. ASRIEL
emerges half-dressed into the storm, followed by two
SERVANTS.

ASRIEL. What is it?

SERVANT 1. Out there! Small boat in difficulty, my lord.

ASRIEL. It's a canoe!

SERVANT 1. Somebody in it, sir. Two people!

ASRIEL. Two children!

SERVANT 2. They're in the water!

SERVANT 1. The current's very strong there!

ASRIEL (*cups hands, shouts*). Make towards the bank! The
river becomes shallow once you leave the centre channel!

Now inside October House, they carry MALCOLM *and*
ALICE, ALICE *holding* LYRA *tight in her arms, filthy,
physically ruined, still carrying* BONNEVILLE's *rucksack.*

Do I know you?

MALCOLM. Malcolm Polstead.
(*Beat.*)
I lent you my canoe…?
(*Beat.*)
La Belle Sauvage?

ASRIEL (*lying*). Of course!
Come in and dry out…

MALCOLM. You gave me your card and said if I –
(*Quoting helpfully.*) 'need your help at any time be sure to
ask'…

ASRIEL. Then I must keep my promise.

MALCOLM. This is Alice.

ASRIEL. Alice.
(*He sees that she is carrying* LYRA.)
Is this your baby, Alice?

ALICE. No!
It's *your* baby!

MALCOLM. It's Lyra...

ASRIEL *goes very still, alert*.

ALICE. Me and Mal rescued her from Gerard Bonneville.

MALCOLM. And her *mother*.

ALICE. And *everybody*!

ASRIEL *backs away from the offered baby*.

ASRIEL. What the hell are you playing at, bringing her here?

ALICE. You think we're *playing*?
You wrote a card saying you'd help,
and by God there is nowhere else she'll be safe!
Playing? If I told you *half* what Mal's done to keep us alive!

ASRIEL. I can't help you. I'm sorry. You need to take this baby and go.

ALICE. You're sorry?

MALCOLM. 'This Baby.'

ASRIEL (*to* SERVANTS). Take these young people to the kitchen.
Give them some breakfast, then send them on their way.
Now!
(*He urges them towards the exit*.)

MALCOLM. What kind of father are you?

ASRIEL. Let's agree I'm a truly terrible one.

MALCOLM. You *said* this was your address if I needed help, you *liar*...

MRS COULTER *enters, post-coital, in* ASRIEL*'s shirt*.

MRS COULTER. I hope you don't mind my borrowing this.

MALCOLM. Why is *she* here?

ASRIEL (*to* SERVANTS). Too late. Get out.

SERVANTS *exit*.

MALCOLM. You said 'Look out for my daughter' so we did!
You said 'Keep her safe from her mother' so we did!

ALICE. We just been through hell and she's here with you!

MALCOLM. What's she doing here?

ASRIEL. Well, until *you* arrived,
I thought it was because we still meant something to one another.
But – (*To* MRS COULTER.) I'm a fool. You *knew* these two would bring the baby here.

MRS COULTER. Where else would they bring her? You have your fingers in every pie.
They stole her from a convent.

MALCOLM. I didn't *steal* her! You took the wrong baby and *then* I took Lyra!
You can't even recognise your own baby!

ALICE. Either of you!

MRS COULTER. You have my baby.
Give her to me.

MALCOLM. No.

ALICE. Try taking her and I'll tear your eyes out of their sockets.

MRS COULTER. Dramatic but over-ambitious.
If you look out there… a CCD motor launch is waiting for me.
I'll call them now and end this pointless discussion.

Impasse.

ASRIEL. Tell these children what you intend for our child, Marisa.
(*Beat.*)
Are you going to be Mummy?
In a little cottage with a nice crisp apron so you don't get milk all down you?

MRS COULTER. I'm going to take her ab/road.

ASRIEL. *Where* abroad?

MRS COULTER. You bastard. You took me to bed / and you…

ASRIEL. Oh I think *you* took *me* to bed, Marisa.

MRS COULTER. We *both* commit adultery but somehow only
  I get disgraced.
  Only *I* have my research fund stopped.

ASRIEL. You're going to give her to the Magisterium,
  which will put you back in their good books once more,
  won't it?
  A gift for the Magisterium, who will surely kill her.

MRS COULTER. No.

ASRIEL. *Yes. We both know that*. The child we made together is
  the subject of a prophecy…

ALICE. You ent handing her over to nobody to die!

ASRIEL.…which could tear them apart.

ALICE (*faces off* MRS COULTER). Come one step nearer Lyra
  and I'll cut your heart right out of your chest…

MALCOLM. She will she'll *kill* you. So will I.

ASRIEL. They're serious.

MALCOLM. We *fucking are. Sorry*.

  Beat.

ASRIEL. Marisa, look at Lyra.

  Everybody looks at LYRA.

  Are you really going to live the rest of your life
  knowing you helped end the life of your own baby?
  (*Beat*.)
  Our baby. Marisa, we made one good thing together.
  Don't hand her over to the Magisterium.
  (*Beat*.)
  You're the cleverest woman in the world. You'll find some
  other way to get all the power you want.
  (*Beat*.)
  Your own clothes must be dry now.

MRS COULTER *thinks. Then goes to* LYRA. *She looks at* LYRA *for a long time, then…*

MRS COULTER. You can have her for now, while she's dribbling and incapable of words. (*To* LYRA.) Let these fools get you upright and walking and sentient. We'll meet again when you can form sentences. Then, we shall talk, you and I. And then we will together accomplish such remarkable things. (*She touches* LYRA *on her cheek. Exits.*)

ALICE (*pointedly ignores* ASRIEL, *turns to* MALCOLM). What now, Mal?

MALCOLM. What Dr Relf said. Scholastic sanctuary. Jordan College.
But I don't know the Latin words. And the flood smashed up *La Belle Sauvage*.

ALICE (*to* ASRIEL). Hear that? The flood smashed up his canoe.
We need to go to Jordan College. We don't know the Latin words.

MALCOLM (*to* ALICE). We got an alethiometer. And Gerard Bonneville's research papers…

ALICE. What about a deal…?

MALCOLM. Sanctuary for / Lyra.

ASRIEL. You've got Gerard Bonneville's research papers – (*He holds out his hand for them…*) May I see them?

ALICE (*holds the rucksack back*). We got to get to Jordan College…

ASRIEL. I'll take you.

ALICE. It's the least you can do, she's *your* bloody baby!

And a sound of gyrocopter blades.

15. A Gyrocopter Ride

A gyrocopter flies. A bird's eye view of a trip back upriver.
The flood is receding. They can see the emerging tops of
buildings as…

MALCOLM. I'm in a gyrocopter! *I'm in a gyrocopter!*

ALICE. Sky's for birds!

BEN. People should be on the earth.

ALICE. You've been a dog for days, Ben. You've settled,
    haven't you?

BEN. Sky's for birds. Water should stay in rivers.

MALCOLM. It *is* now. The water's going down *fast… Look!*
    The – (*Mispronounces.*) *cupola of* St Paul's!

ALICE. I'm happy you've settled as a dog.

BEN. If you're happy, I'm happy.

MALCOLM. Our country's got a lot of trees, hasn't it?

BEN. I bloody love trees!

ASTA. Me too!

ALICE. What's that pale-green field?

MALCOLM. Early wheat. Somebody's got a big bonfire going
    there!

ALICE. I can smell the smoke! Right up here! I bloody love the
    smell of woodsmoke!

MALCOLM. Me too!
    (*Beat.*)
    Sorry.

ALICE. Sorry for what?

MALCOLM. For the Sleeping Beauty incident… I just wanted
    to… you know…

ALICE. Mal. We're not gonna do the kissing stuff.

MALCOLM. Okay.

ALICE. That's not our stuff.

MALCOLM. Right.

ALICE. We're friends.

MALCOLM. Sweet.

ALICE (*beat*). And... if you want to kiss people, you bloody
    ask them!

MALCOLM. Right.
    (*Beat.*)
    Look! Ahead!

As a wonderful rainbow forms.

ALICE. What?
    (*Immense joy as she sees.*) Oh!

MALCOLM. *Rainbow!*

ALICE. Bloody *perfect* rainbow!

MALCOLM (*to* LYRA). It's a rainbow. A rainbow is an optical
    phenomenon which occurs when a light wave hits a water
    droplet –

ASTA. Lecturing.

MALCOLM. Don't care – at exactly forty-two degrees and
    separates into red, orange, yellow, green...

MALCOLM *and* ALICE *and* ASTA *and* BEN....blue, indigo,
    violet...

16. Jordan College

The rainbow illuminates a crowd in Jordan College quadrangle.
NUGENT, HANNAH, CLUNY, YASMIN, PAPADIMITRIOU
in flapping gowns, holding onto escaping mortar boards.

CLUNY. It's a gyropcopter!

YASMIN. In *this* / weather?

PAPADIMITRIOU. First I've seen since / the flood!

CLUNY. It's a four-/rotor!

PAPADIMITROU. It looks like Asriel's!

YASMIN. Somebody's with him, / I think!

CLUNY. It's two children!

PAPADIMITROU. Is it the two we're looking for?

CLUNY. If it's the two we're / looking for –

NUGENT. He's landing on the college / bloody roof!

CLUNY. Is the baby with them?

    ALICE, MALCOLM, LYRA *and* ASRIEL *arrive as…*

MALCOLM (*hands* LYRA *to* NUGENT). Sir, the baby you put
in the care of the nuns at Godstow Priory.
Delivered safe and sound.

ASRIEL. Lord Nugent, Master of Jordan…
*Secundum legem de refugia scholasticorum
protectionem tegimentumque huius collegii
pro filia mea Lyra nomine reposco!*

NUGENT. You want *scholastic* sanctuary? For a *child*?

ASRIEL. She's *my daughter*, Tom.

NUGENT. But… she's not exactly a scholar!

ALICE. You'll have to make her into one then, won't you?

MALCOLM. And, she comes with *this*.
(*He takes the bag off* ALICE.) An alethiometer.

NUGENT. Well, this is very interesting, Asriel, but which of *us* do you think is going to look after her?

The DONS *look at each other uneasily.*

ALICE. I will.

NUGENT. And who are you?

ALICE. Alice Parslow. Experienced Nappy-changer. You pay me… you give me a room – I'll look after her.

MALCOLM. Mrs Brenda Polstead at The Trout, Godstow, could give you a reference…

ASRIEL. The perfect solution to your quandary, Nugent.

NUGENT. The child's safety is guaranteed.
Asriel, can we give you lunch?

NUGENT, DONS *and* ASRIEL *all exit for lunch, leaving* HANNAH *alone.*

HANNAH. Well done, Malcolm… and 'Sandra Parsons'.

MALCOLM. Thank you, Dr Relf.

HANNAH *exits, following the other* DONS, *leaving* ALICE *and* MALCOLM *alone with* LYRA.

ALICE. He's taken the papers.

MALCOLM. You're not coming back to The Trout?

ALICE. Lyra needs looking after. You and your mum'll manage.

MALCOLM. Yeh.
(*Beat.*)
I best go let her know I'm alright.

ALICE. Yeh.

Beat.

MALCOLM. Well. Bye then.

ALICE. Bye.

MALCOLM *goes to go.*

Mal?

MALCOLM. Yeh?

ALICE. I'll visit.

MALCOLM. You will?

ALICE. Course. I'll come for dinner. It'll taste all the better knowing you're the one washing the pots afterwards.

They laugh. They want to say something else, like 'I'll miss you' but they can't. Just the thought makes a big hole in their conversation.

In the space between ALICE *and* MALCOLM, ASTA *and* BEN *nuzzle each other. The lights fade.*

The End.

FRANKENSTEIN
Patrick Sandford
Adapted from Mary Shelley

GREAT EXPECTATIONS
Nick Ormerod and Declan Donnellan
Adapted from Charles Dickens

THE HAUNTING
Hugh Janes
Adapted from Charles Dickens

HIS DARK MATERIALS
Nicholas Wright
Adapted from Philip Pullman

THE HOUND OF THE BASKERVILLES
Steven Canny & John Nicholson
Adapted from Arthur Conan Doyle

JANE EYRE
Polly Teale
Adapted from Charlotte Brontë

JEEVES AND WOOSTER IN PERFECT NONSENSE
The Goodale Brothers
Adapted from P.G. Wodehouse

THE JUNGLE BOOK
Stuart Paterson
Adapted from Rudyard Kipling

KES
Lawrence Till
Adapted from Barry Hines

THE MASSIVE TRAGEDY OF MADAME BOVARY
John Nicholson & Javier Marzan
Adapted from Gustave Flaubert

MY FAMILY AND OTHER ANIMALS
Janys Chambers
Adapted from Gerald Durrell

NORTHANGER ABBEY
Tim Luscombe
Adapted from Jane Austen

PERSUASION
Mark Healy
Adapted from Jane Austen

PRIDE AND PREJUDICE* (*SORT OF)
Isobel McArthur
Adapted from Jane Austen

THE RAILWAY CHILDREN
Mike Kenny
Adapted from E. Nesbit

SENSE AND SENSIBILITY
Mark Healy
Adapted from Jane Austen

SWALLOWS AND AMAZONS
Helen Edmundson and Neil Hannon
Adapted from Arthur Ransome

THE THREE MUSKETEERS
John Nicholson & Le Navet Bete
Adapted from Alexander Dumas

TREASURE ISLAND
Stuart Paterson
Adapted from Robert Louis Stevenson

THE WIND IN THE WILLOWS
Mike Kenny
Adapted from Kenneth Grahame

WHISKY GALORE
Philip Goulding
Adapted from Compton Mackenzie

www.nickhernbooks.co.uk

facebook.com/nickhernbooks

twitter.com/nickhernbooks

Our Bobby: Or A Sea Gift

Grace Stebbing

"OUR BOBBY;"

OR,

A SEA GIFT.

BY
GRACE STEBBING,
AUTHOR OF "WILD KATHLEEN," "WALTER BENN," ETC.

LONDON:
THE BOOK SOCIETY, 28, PATERNOSTER ROW.

To

Mary Stebbing.

In Memoriam.

CONTENTS.

vii

Only a face in a crowd, only a look and a touch,
Only a thoughtful, kindly act; truly it was not much.
But the lame man dreamt of that face, dreamt of that
    touch and look,
And, learning belief in love, his pitiful doubts forsook.
Then leave your preaching awhile, my friend, and
    show your faith in deeds,
Winning the sorrowful ones to God, by caring for
    their needs.

"OUR BOBBY;" OR, A SEA GIFT.

CHAPTER I.

"ONLY OUR BOBBY."

TWO women standing together talking, at the outskirts of the village of Summerton: one, a stately-looking individual, with a calm sensible face, and her person clothed sedately in a plain, untrimmed black silk; the other, a bustling, red-cheeked village body in a lilac cotton gown, and a check red-and-green shawl lightly pinned round her.

"Well, ma'am," said the cotton-gown

body, glibly, "it's not to wonder at, of
course, that you don't know the lassie
yonder, seein' as you're a stranger; but
there's ne'er a one belonging to the place,
gentle or simple, for the three miles round
the neighbourhood, nor right away to
market town for the matter of that, that
doesn't know her, and more than that, I'll
make bold to say as isn't the better for
knowing our Bobby."

"Our Bobby!" repeated the new housekeeper at the Hall with fresh surprise,
and turning from her companion to have
another look at a young girl of fifteen or
sixteen, sitting in a field close by, with a
large circle of children seated round her,
all busily engaged with fingers, eyes, and
ears.   The group was as pretty a sight
as Mrs. Mitters, or any one else, had ever
seen.

"But why 'Bobby'?" she repeated.
"Why call the little maid 'Bobby'?" she
asked wonderingly.   "Did her mother have
her christened by that queer name, like a
boy, for a fancy?"

"Goodness knows what her mother had the dear child christened," was the sighing answer. "She had a mother certainly, that much she does remember; but neither she, nor no one else as we can hear of, can

tell who that mother was, nor yet what she'd had her little one named."

"Dear me!" ejaculated Mrs. Mitters, "was she found?"

"Ay, found, to be sure she was, on the beach, thirteen years ago; some folk say as they suppose as a ship went down off this

coast, but that's as it may be. Anyhow,
nothing an' nobody was saved, if so, but
this child in her little night-dress and a
large shawl, flung up on to the beach in
an empty barrel. Popped in at the last
moment, in a forlorn hope to save it,
Parson said, belike; but I've my notions
how the baby come there, and other folks
are welcome to theirs; and anyhow it was
in a barrel as it was washed ashore, tied in
tight, and when it was brought to, poor
little lamb, it opened its big blue eyes quite
wide all at once, and said, 'Mumma, Dadda,
Bobby awake;' and from that day to this
'Bobby' she has been called."

"Poor little lassie!" again ejaculated the
housekeeper, as though that last fact was
the crowning misfortune in the young girl's
fate. "But surely," she added, after a
moment's pause, "surely she must have got
some prettier name than that to suit her
pretty face."

The village gossip looked quite taken
aback for a moment, as she exclaimed—
"Prettier! why we all think 'Bobby' so

pretty that half the children hereabouts
are christened Bobby now, after her."

"Dear, dear, you never say such a
thing!" ejaculated worthy Mrs. Mitters, as
solemnly as if she had been told of some
national calamity.

"Dear, dear," she repeated. "Only to
think of that, now!"

Mrs. Granby laughed. "Well, ma'am,
there's Taffys for Wales, Paddys for Ire-
land, Sandys for your own country, why
not Bobbys for Summerton or Downfells?"

But Mrs. Mitters did not condescend to
laugh, nor so much as even to smile at the
irreverent small joke. She harped back
instead on the young waif's name. "Did
no one ask her, little lost lamb, what she
was called?"

Mrs. Granby tossed her head scornfully
at such a question. She did not forgive
the cool indifference shown towards her
ill-timed jest; it was her turn to be con-
temptuous now.

"Ask, indeed, do you say, ma'am! My

goodness, we ain't sillies no more than
some other folks who may think themselves
so wise. Scores o' folks asked her scores
o' times, and she always answered in the
same way—'Dadda's darling, Mumma's
Bobby.' "

"Mamma's baby, she must have meant,"
said Mrs. Mitters thoughtfully.

"Very like," was the off-hand answer.
"Many another has said that same. Good-
day to you, ma'am."

And Mrs. Granby walked off. She had
been all eagerness to give a new-comer the
whole short history of the lovely young
girl in the field; but the prospect of giving
it to a person who took so very long to get
over the mere outset of the name, dismayed
even her untiring tongue and turn for idleness. She marched off to her own cottage,
or rather to the paling between her garden
and her neighbour's. The Naylors lived
next door, and the young wife, Lucy, was
hanging out her wash. Mrs. Granby leant
over the paling, chattering to her of "the
new old Prose" come to the Hall, till

the husbands of both women came in to tea, and found none ready for them.

" I wish to goodness as you'd take a leaf out of our Bobby's book," grumbled Charles Granby, looking at the fireless grate and comfortless kitchen.

"Our Bobby, indeed," retorted Mrs. Granby, proportionably cross in that she knew she was to blame. " Our Bobby's got no husband to fash after, the better luck for her, poor young thing. She'll learn soon enough, when she has, that the more she does the more she may do, and be found fault with for all."

Charles Granby ignored the unjust, implied accusation flung at him, and replied to the first part of the speech—

" It will be a lucky young fellow that will one day win our Bobby, and he'll just have as handy a wife as he'll have a bonny one. There she be, as I come by just now, out in the fields as usual with the little 'uns all around her, and ne'er a one o' them little or big, 'ourn nor none, let to talk nor listen wi'out a bit o' work o' some kind in's hand. She won't learn the next set o' villagers to grow up idle gossips, I'll be bound."

And then the justly angered husband walked out of his dreary home again, resolved to take a most foolish revenge on his wife by wasting his own money and health in the alehouse, drinking a quantity of beer in place of the tea he had to wait for.

Charles Granby had walked the length of the village, and just reached the "Cross Keys," when he felt a touch on his elbow, and, turning, exclaimed with a smile,—

"Why to be sure, lassie, how ye startled me! What is it ye can be wanting wi' me, I wonder?"

That Miss Bobby did want something was evident enough. There was such a very pleading look in the large earnest blue eyes that were raised to his face, as their owner said timidly, after a moment's hesitation,—

"I thought perhaps—please—you'd be so very good as walk back with me to

your garden, to show me those new straw-
berry plants of yours, and then——"

"Hey well, and then?" asked the farm
labourer kindly enough but quickly. "What
would ye have with me after that, lassie?"

"Why then—if—if—you don't mind—
I've taken a fancy that I'd like to have
tea with you and your wife this evening."

The colour flushed for a moment into
the man's face, and he turned his eyes back
to the public-house. But it was only for
an instant, then he let a growing frown
fade into a smile, as he answered,—

"Well, well! Of all wheedling little
lassies! But I suppose I must give you
your way, although you know, as well's I
do, that if you'd seen e'er another man instead o' me a walking into th' ale-house as
early as this, to spend his evening there,
it 'ud ha' been with him an' his wife as
you'd ha' fancied to take your tea, 'stead o'
with us. Say now, truth down, ain't I
guessed clean right?"

But all the answer the young girl
seemed to think it prudent to make to

this interrogative speech was a gentle, "But you will take me back to tea with you, won't you?"

"To ask!" exclaimed her companion, laughing. "When ye know yourself, none better, that there ain't not the roughest, nor the curmudgeonliest about the place, as ever gives ye a 'Nay' about aught. Come along, come your ways, wilful that they are.

"Ay, ay, lassie," he added resolutely, "ye needn't to shake your head and look at me like that, for good and pretty and clever your ways may be, I'm no denying that, but woman-like wilful they are, all the same, and I'm not the one to say as I don't believe ye know it."

And then, with a little backward shrug of the shoulders directed at the public-house, he marched back up the long straggling street again, with the fair, slim girl by his side, who seemed so strangely out of place in that semi-fishing, semi-agricultural village on the south-west coast.

In the present day her strange, short

history would be an impossible one. Fifty years ago things were different. The vessel went down with every one and everything, as Mrs. Granby had said, with the exception of a desolate baby, who was washed up to an out-of-the-way poor village, with no richer or more intelligent inhabitants than the illiterate farmers and their labourers. A university rector, it was true, belonged to the place, but he was old, indolent, and an absentee, and the curate in charge was equally old and indolent, and only too glad not to be "bothered."

Few letters and fewer newspapers travelled to or from that little forgotten spot of the globe; and the lovely, desolate little creature, who, in these days, would be a nine days' source of interest, possibly adopted by some grandee, at any rate comfortably provided for in some school, was left to the tender mercies of a set of rough and ignorant villagers.

They, however, forthwith adopted her between them, by which arrangement she

had no settled abode anywhere, but homes
everywhere, as the housekeeper's informant had truly said, in any house or
cottage that she chose to enter for three
miles round that coast.

A few weeks in one abode, a few weeks in
another, every one vying with neighbours as
to who should keep her with them longest.
And she grew up so winsome and so bonny,
that for the father whom she had lost she
became everybody's darling, and for the
mother, " Our Bobby."

When she was about sixteen, however,
its long-absent owners came back to
Deepmoat Hall, and then came many a
change.

CHAPTER II.

"OUR BOBBY'S" FAIRY TALE.

HE housekeeper at the Hall was so impressed with the sight of the fair young girl, whom she had seen the day after her own first arrival in the neighbourhood, that she bestowed many more thoughts upon her than she had done in her life before upon any one of the troublesome race of lassies.

But some days passed before she saw her again. The long-disused house had made serious calls upon time and thought,

21

ere it was got into fair order, and the housekeeper felt able to make holiday.

At last, however, one afternoon, she decided that she had properly earned a rest, and putting on her bonnet Mrs. Mitters crossed the park, and turned into the field where she had first made acquaintance with the young stranger's lovely face.

Finding a splendid tree at the farther side, she spread her shawl on the ground under it, and sat down to think of many things, but more than all of the golden-haired girl; orphaned and homeless, but so abounding in joy and goodness and gladness, that even the sorrows of others seemed to melt before her feet.

In the midst of her meditations the housekeeper fell asleep, and when she awoke she heard the sound of a child crying, and some soft voice comforting the little one, on the other side of the large dark-shadowed tree. She lay quite still, partly because she was yet too drowsy to move, partly because she found the gentle voice almost as soothing as the child seemed to do.

After a minute the crying ceased, and a somewhat penitent voice sobbed out,—

"But, Bobby, it is bad, isn't it, to feel one always gets the worst of everything?"

"Very bad," said a tender voice; "and so, to make up, now I'll give you a little bit of the best of everything, if you like. You shall sit in my lap, and I'll tell you a little story all to yourself, shall I?"

But the question was so little needed that the questioner hardly had time to utter it before the child had seized her round the neck, and kissed and hugged her almost breathless. The next minute the tale began as follows; Bobby on one side of the tree, with the child in her lap; Mrs. Mitters, the housekeeper, on the other, seated at her ease on her shawl, with her back resting comfortably against the broad trunk.

"What is the story called?" asked the child.

"Ah! I must think," was the laughing answer, and after a few moments' thought she replied—"Well, suppose we call it the

' Fairy of the River Glen.'"

"Yes, that sounds quite pretty," was the satisfied answer. "And so now, does it begin with the fairy, and was she finely dressed?"

"No, Nettie dear. It begins with a little girl, and she was dressed in poor, shabby clothes, with no hat to shield her head from the sun's hot rays, and her shoes were almost too old to guard her poor little toes from the sharp, hard stones. This little girl lay sobbing by the side of a running brook that dimpled with sparkling smiles, and danced over the pebbles that lay beneath its clear waters.

"There were some big grey stones in the middle of the little brook's bed, and as it tossed and tumbled over these, and splashed the branches of the trees that bent above it, the little girl could hear soft laughter ringing from the falling drops, and the water-lilies growing in the quiet bend whispered to the reeds that grew beside them,—

"'Our world is a happy world, and beautiful.'

"'Happy! Beautiful!' sighed little Nelly. 'But yes, your world is happy and beautiful, I know, and so is Dora's world, she says; but my world is miserable, and oh! so very wretched and dirty and ugly.'

"And Nelly's tears fell faster, and rolled down her cheeks, and dropped into the beautiful brook that curved away in ever-widening circles from where the hot, salt drops fell, as though they were, in their sadness, a pain to it, from which it longed to get away.

"Nelly's eyes were filled with tears, but all of a sudden she fancied that she could see through their mist a strange something, rising up through the water. She wiped away her tears, and looked more earnestly. Then she sat up, and her eyes grew wide with wonder.

"'Something,' indeed, there was, rising gently from the sparkling brook, and a most marvellous something too. After gazing for a few moments, Nelly saw with delight a lovely fairy hovering over the water. Her dress was all of the glistening spray, and a wreath of blue forget-me-nots crowned hair that shone like the golden buttercups in the sunlight. She had ear-rings of the soft green moss, and a wand of the silvery drops. From her little white feet the waters fell in all the colours of the rainbow.

" Nelly clasped her hands for joy, and exclaimed—'Oh! beautiful fairy, stay. Live with me always, and my world too shall be happy and beautiful.'

" The fairy sighed and smiled as she replied—'Ah! dear child, that is what all people say when they first see me; but they generally get tired of me so soon, if I pay them a visit, and you have never even asked me to spend so much as half an hour with you before.'

"Nelly stared with astonishment as she said—'Why, how could I? I have never even seen you or heard of you before.'

"'Have you not?' said the fairy gently.

'That is strange, too, for your little
friend, Dora, has me with her nearly
always. But never mind the past now;
for the future I trust that we also may be
friends. And now I will show you some
pictures in my water book. They will
amuse you, and may perhaps be of some
use to you also.'

"As the fairy spoke she touched the little
girl's eyes with her wand, and suddenly
Nelly saw lying before her a beautiful
book bound in crystal. The fairy turned
to the first picture. It was a very simple
one, but Nelly thought it both pretty and
pleasant to look at.

"There was a little three-roomed
thatched cottage, with common wooden
bedsteads, and common mugs and plates,
and rough tables and chairs; there were
no nice warm carpets on the floors, and
only one of the rooms had even a tiny
bit of rug before the hearth. But all was
whole, and neat, and clean.

"'What a dear, nice little place. How
comfortable it looks!' sighed Nelly,
looking longingly at the cottage.

" 'That is because I live there,' said the lovely fairy, with a bright smile; and she turned to the next picture—a picture of another cottage, but instead of bending over this one with pleasure, as she had over the last, the moment Nelly's eyes rested on it she covered them with her hands, crying out,—

" 'Oh! please, dear fairy, turn quickly to the next page, that I may not have to look at that ugly picture again. It is just like my miserable home, and since I saw you I have been so happy that I had nearly forgotten there was such a dismal place.'

" 'But, dear child, it is surely better to remember that you have a home?' urged the fairy kindly. 'For you will be hungry soon, and must go there to get your dinner.'

" 'It is sure to be a nasty dinner. I always get the smallest and boniest fish, and the worst potatoes, and the least salt,' grumbled Nelly, the fairy's words reminding her of her daily troubles and complaints.

"But, as the little girl spoke, the lovely bright fairy seemed fading away from her into the air. Terribly afraid that she was about to lose her beautiful companion, and would never see her again, Nelly forgot all about the 'nasty dinner,' and exclaimed,—

"'Oh! beautiful lady, come back to me, please come back to me, and show me some more of your pictures.'

"And, even as she was pleading, she felt the fairy wand touch her eyes again, and she once more saw the fairy, and the crystal book shining in the sunlight.

"'For one minute look again at these two pictures, little one,' said the fairy; and turning back to the first, Nelly saw a child about her own age, and looking very much like her own happy little friend, Dora, carefully sweeping the floor. The picture changed a little. Nelly saw the same child tenderly washing her baby brother, and singing a pretty song to it the while.

"Again that picture changed. But still

Nelly saw the same tidy, bright-faced child, and now she was holding to her mother a great bunch of fresh wild flowers she had gathered to put on father's supper table, to make it bright and cheerful. And Nelly saw that her beautiful fairy was ever at the child's side, and shedding a shining joy from herself over the little face.

"Then the second picture appeared once more—a cottage built quite like the first, with the same number of chairs and tables, mugs and plates, and beds, as the first, but all dirty, and dusty, and ragged, and miserable. A poor tired mother was in the cottage with a crying baby in her arms, and a little girl like Nelly, who could have helped her, was lying idle all the day, grumbling by the seashore or the running brook; and the merriment of the one and the glory of the other were useless to her, for no glad fairy shed shining joy over her dirty, discontented little face.

"The fairy turned the gleaming leaves of the book to a third picture,—the people

of the first picture sitting at their dinner.
The mother got up for a moment, and,
while she was not looking, the bright
little girl changed her own plate of potatoes for her mother's, for the mother had
kept the worst for herself.

"They turned to the fourth picture.
The tired mother and the crying baby, and
the dirty-faced little girl, were also having
their dinner.

"'Give me those fishes you have given
to Jamie; I won't have these nasty little
things,' cries the little girl like Nelly, as
she pushes her plate crossly from her, and
snatches at what she thinks are the best
on the table.

"And Nelly blushed deeply. She knew
then what the pictures meant, and she
said: 'Oh, dear fairy! tell me your
name, and stay with me, and help me to
grow like Dora.'

"And the fairy smiled brightly as she
replied, 'My name is Contentment, and I
will live with you.'"

The fairy-tale teller ceased, and there

was silence. At last a voice said, little above a whisper, " Yes, Bobby, dear Bobby ! and I know too what the pictures meant, and what the story means too. Oh, Bobby ! I didn't think I'd been so bad. I will try to have Contentment live with me too ; and I'll go home now and wash my face, and help mother to put baby to bed."

"And I'll go up to the Hall and ask the new housekeeper for some sweet new milk for your suppers," said the little village spirit of peace. And the two went away together, and Mrs. Mitters rose and slipped back the nearer way, quicker than she had thought her feet could move, to be in time to grant the desired gift.

CHAPTER III.

VERY SURPRISING NEWS.

WELVE years before the large vessel, on which the child Bobby had been a passenger, had been wrecked almost within sight of the villagers of Summerton and Downfells, the owner of Deep-moat Hall had been killed in the hunting-field.

A few weeks later, his young widow had left a place now become so terrible to her, and, taking with her her little son, then an infant not yet two years old, had wandered about the world seeking ease for an aching heart. It is probable that the mutual love of herself and her boy, and the care of his education, did even

more for her in softening grief than
change of scene; and when Harbston
Deacon at length expressed a strong desire
to return to his own estates, Mrs. Deacon
gave a glad assent.

Time makes so many changes. The
place she had fled from so desperately,
because it had been the scene of such
short-lived joy, she now felt as eager to
return to, because it was within its bounds
that the three happiest years of her life
had been passed.

"And we owe the estates and your
tenants many, many duties," said the lady,
with a repentant sigh, "which we have
sorely neglected during all these bygone
years.

"But," the mother added after a moment, affectionately, "you are not to
blame, my son. It has all been my doing,
and my fault."

Of course Harbston Deacon would not
admit so much. But he did confess that
a feeling of duty was added to his other
anxieties to return home.

The word "home" struck a deeper chord in his mother's heart than in his own, and silence fell between them during the last hour of their last day's journey, until the post horses drew up before the great doors of Deepmoat Hall, and the young squire and his mother were received with all due courtesy and welcome by their new housekeeper, Mrs. Mitters. That worthy woman smoothed down her long laced apron, with hands that trembled with joyful hope of coming pleasure, in her fresh sphere of duties, as she looked intelligently at the faces of her new master and mistress.

"I only hope, madam," she said earnestly, "that we all hereabouts, people and places, will be able to please you so much that we shall have the happiness to keep you in our midst for many a future year to come."

Mrs. Deacon smiled kindly at the speaker. "I thank you for your wish, Mrs. Mitters. I assure you I have very little fear that I shall feel tempted to go roving again, in search of any earthly good which I am not much more likely to find here. But you must not begin by fostering our selfishness, I pray. My son and I have returned as much at the call of duty as of inclination. We have been away from our own home too long, and we have come back at length strong in the great desire, not to be pleased ourselves, but so to please as to benefit all about us, and to repair the great wrong we must have done by our lengthened absence."

Mrs. Mitters raised her eyes eagerly at those last words, and opened her lips, as quickly closing them again, however, as though second thoughts appeared more prudent. Her manner excited her mistress's curiosity, and she said in a tone of friendly encouragement,—

"There is something that you wish to say to us, Mrs. Mitters, I can see. I hope neither I nor my son are so formidable as to frighten our own people from speaking out their thoughts to us."

"Ah, no, ma'am," was the apologetic

answer. "And indeed I am sure you are not that, only there are some things that perhaps one should not say to the most affable master and mistress. Though I do trust I'm taking no very great liberty, if—if—I tell you—that you need to have less anxiety about the people on these estates, than many should have, who have never been away from theirs for a day."

There was something in the house-keeper's voice as she uttered these words which tenfold increased her hearers' curiosity. There was evidently some meaning hidden in the short speech, far deeper than appeared on the surface. Harbston Deacon, as well as his mother, came more forward, and it was he this time who put the question,—

"How comes that, Mrs. Mitters? How come we to be so favoured? When I was a young boy I believe my mother used to be a good deal troubled, by our agent's accounts of the lawlessness, and idleness, and ignorance, of my tenants. They had anything but a name for being better than their neighbours in those days, I am afraid."

"They had no fairy child amongst them then," said the housekeeper in a hushed, solemn voice, and with a glance around her to see that all the doors of the large reception room were shut.

Whatever her own superstitious beliefs might be, as to the real nature of the beautiful and singularly gifted young alien of Downfells, the canny Scotch housekeeper was perfectly alive to the very troublesome consequences of letting such notions get entrance into minds not so amenable to discipline.

It was right that her employers should be made acquainted with her suspicions, but by no rule of propriety or justice was she bound to take the housemaids and footmen and scullery-maid into her confidence. If they could be made to suppose that "Our Bobby" was a poor little orphaned passenger saved from a lost vessel, so much the better; but Mrs. Mitters, who had not been there when the vessel was wrecked,

and the cask flung up by the wild waves
with its baby occupant, believed something
else as strongly as the Scotch turn for the
supernatural, fifty years ago, enabled her
to do.

The child who had so softened the
rugged natures of those who had rescued
and cherished her, the girl who was so
teaching and training those about her that
the sweet ennobling influence was spreading far and wide, was to her imagination
a fairy child, a being from the invisible
regions mid earth and heaven, sent to
bless and purify a hitherto dark, forgotten
corner of the world.

Mrs. Mitters had been six weeks at
Deepmoat Hall when Harbston Deacon
and his mother returned to their long-
abandoned home, and every day of the
six weeks had brought or given her some
fresh evidence of the benign and singular
influence of this blue-eyed, golden-haired,
storm-spared " Bobby."

But the first feeling aroused in the mind
of Mrs. Deacon by the words of the house-

keeper was one of scornful annoyance.
Between twenty and thirty years ago that
especial neighbourhood had been tolerably
free from a belief in witches and such-like
folks, even when their existence was held
as an orthodox article of faith in many
places of the kingdom.

It would be indeed annoying, then, to
find credulity had grown in those parts
when it was fading away from others.
And to have a grave, sensible-looking
person like their own confidential servant,
too, nourishing the idea, was really too
vexatious! Altogether, it is little to be
wondered at that the lady's voice betrayed
a degree of impatience when she at last
exclaimed,—

"What can you mean? Whatever can
you mean?"

"Ay, indeed, this is quite delightful;
pray do explain what you mean," said
Harbston Deacon, laughing. His senti-
ments on the subject were widely different
to those of his mother, notwithstanding
their almost constant accord on all matters

of any importance. But the woman's queer little speech did sound so much as if she forgot that her new master was a grown-up man, and rather beyond the age for frightening with bogies, or rewarding with tales of " Jack and the Beanstalk " and " Little Goody Two Shoes."

However, neither the sternness of the lady nor the laughter of the gentleman had any effect in disturbing the calmness of their companion. Mrs. Mitters had not been a housekeeper for nearly twenty years to be "flustered," as she would herself have called it, by trifles. Simply smoothing down her laced apron again, over her second best black silk, she said in a tone even more grave and emphatic than before,—

" Yes, ma'am; yes, sir. It is just that I mean, and nothing more, and nothing less. Twenty years ago, and fifteen years ago, this place had not the blessing of a fairy child in it; and if this Miss Bobby isn't one, then what is she ? "

" Just the very thing we should like

to know," said the young man, greatly
interested and amused. " Whose child is
she ? "

" Ah! sir," was the hushed answer,
" that is what no one knows. She came
out of the sea in a tub."

" What !" shouted Harbston Deacon.
And then he suddenly drew his lips together in a great effort of self-control.
But it was no good. Those rebellious lips
burst asunder again, as suddenly as they
had been closed, with a great explosion of
laughter, and for some moments both the
women looked quite alarmed, as if they
thought he was going to have a fit. The
expressions of their faces so much further
increased his risibility, that he almost
thought so himself at last. Relief came
from a most unexpected quarter.

There was a sharp tap at the door.
There had been three before, but no one
had heard them through the laughter.
Then impatience got into the waiter's
knuckles, and made the fourth tap too
loud to be ignored. Mrs. Deacon gave

her son a half-beseeching glance, that he
would try to restrain his superabundant
mirth before another of his new servants,
and then called, " Come in ! "

A young footman opened the door, and,
bowing to the lady, turned to Mrs. Mitters
with the deprecatory remark,—

" Please, ma'am, I wouldn't have come
disturbing, only it's for Miss Bobby, she's
waiting for it herself."

The mother and son exchanged quick
glances. The fact was, they now for the
first time actually realized the possible existence of such an individual. The housekeeper's association of the name with
fairy-land had put both together out of
the realms of their comprehension. But
a Miss Bobby who was waiting for something, to be supplied by their own housekeeper, was evidently visible and tangible
in some shape or other.

Mrs. Deacon had tried to get credible
information from the woman in vain, she
determined now to try the man.

" And pray," she said, as she stepped

forward nearer to the door, "and pray,
can you tell me, then, who is this Miss
Bobby?"

The footman stared at his new mistress, and looked puzzled. "Who is she,
ma'am? who is Miss Bobby?"

"Yes, my good fellow, to be sure,"
was the half-impatient answer. "I have
asked nothing very difficult to answer, I
suppose. Who is this Miss Bobby, who
is waiting down below?"

"Well, ma'am," said the man, looking
no whit less puzzled what to say because his mistress had declared her belief
that she had asked nothing difficult to
reply to—"Well, ma'am, you see, she's
just our Bobby, that's what she is, and
she isn't nothing more, only as there isn't
ne'er a one on us as wouldn't lay his head
down willin' for her to tread on, if so be
as she'd like to do it, which it's the last
thing as she would, though."

"I should hope so," said Mr. Deacon,
with laudable solemnity. "But if you
can give us only such meagre information

as to who Miss Bobby is, you can, I suppose, at least tell us where she came
from ? "

"Oh! yes, sir," with alacrity, as if the
man were quite thankful to have got
a question this time that he could give
a full answer to. "Oh, yes, that's easy
told, because you see, sir, she just come
out of the sea in the old cask, which———"

But what was to come after that
"which," no one could tell but the man
himself, for this second confirmation of
the housekeeper's statement was altogether too much for both his astonished
auditors. They neither of them felt in the
least inclined to be angry this time, or to
laugh, they were too utterly bewildered;
and while the man-servant ventured to
step up to his immediate superior, and in
a low voice delivered his errand to her,
Harbston Deacon went up to his mother,
and said, in a manner half serious, half
gay,—

"Mother dear, I confess at last that
you were right. Our rapid journeyings

of late have decidedly been too much for us. We are evidently both asleep and dreaming hard. When you wake up, please awake me."

Mrs. Deacon raised her eyes to her son with a grave smile. "I feel with you, my dear boy, that we must assuredly both be dreaming. But as I have a very great impatience to wake up, I am determined to see and hear as much at once as I can about our housekeeper's fairy child, this Miss Bobby."

So saying, Mrs. Deacon once more turned to her servants, and asked, "What is it the young girl has come for? Anything that I can give her?"

"To be sure," said Mrs. Mitters, with her gravest housekeeper's air. "You cannot think as I would presume, ma'am, to take upon me to give away your things without your leave, now you are on the spot to say what should or should not be!"

Mrs. Mitters looked so solemnly aggrieved at being supposed capable of

taking such a liberty, that Mrs. Deacon
had to relieve her injured feelings with
numerous assurances, before she could
get answers to the questions she had just
asked.

"It's not for herself, you must know,
ma'am, that Miss Bobby ever comes begging," said the housekeeper at last.
"That's one of the strange parts of her
story. For all so young as she is, she
already earns her own living, and has
done, the tenants tell me, ever since she
was nine years old. It was her not liking
to eat the bread of charity and idleness
that first put the other folks about upon
thinking to work honestly, I'm told."

"Well, indeed," said Mr. Harbston
Deacon, "fairy child, or human child, this
queerly-named Miss Bobby is evidently
something out of the common. Come,
mother dear, let us go and ask herself
what we can do to show our appreciation
of her good offices among our tenants."

So saying, the young man opened the
door for his mother to pass, and followed

her and Mrs. Mitters to the side entrance
of the Hall, where a young girl stood,
dressed in a dark blue linsey-woolsey
dress, and a broad-brimmed straw hat.

She had a little white plate in her hand,
which she quickly held forward, as she
heard the approaching steps, and raised
the bent face with a bright smile.

But the plate sank to her side again,
and the smile gave place to a timid flush,
when she saw the strangers. She at once
guessed their identity.

"I beg your pardon," she began in her
soft, clear voice, "for coming here without
leave, but there is a poor fisherman's very
old wife lying ill just now, in the village
down below, and the only thing she seems
able to eat is a little fresh bread and
butter. I hope you will not be angry
with my coming to beg one or two small
slices for her."

"Angry! my dear child," said Mrs.
Deacon, in a tone of much emotion, as
she gazed at the fair, sweet face before
her. "How should I dare be angry with

you for doing the Lord's work. I have heard once or twice that my son's estate here was blessed with a ministering spirit, but I gave little heed to the report."

"And need not," replied that sweet, low voice. "Not all that I can do,—and ah! it is so little, only just what love can think of,—if it were tenfold as much, it could not repay what has been done for me."

"Done for you?" said Mrs. Deacon questioningly.

"Yes, madam," came the earnest reply; and then the deep, beautiful blue eyes were raised to the lady's face, as the girl spoke.

"I have no family or kindred, no home, no name, no money, no claim to anything. The sea spared my life, and swallowed up all else. And yet I have a hundred homes, fathers and mothers, brothers and sisters, throughout the whole length and breadth of this estate. From the day when the sea cast me up on to the shores of this most beautiful place, until I learnt

D

to know and think, the best of everything, even to the best of love, was lavished upon the helpless, unknown, unclaimed baby, who had nothing to give in return but her helpless ' Thank you. ' "

"And such a crowd of blessings upon the place besides," burst in such an impetuous voice just behind her that she and every one else started, "that the place as was going head foremost, at a hard gallop, into the black pit, now dares to remember that there is a sommat beyond the blue sky, and a hereafter. We found her, ma'am, in an old cask, and the sea seemed to our eyes to throw the old cask ashore; but it's not my belief alone, that that there cask came downards afore it touched salt water."

A slight smile hovered across the lips of Harbston Deacon. He had observed the care which his new housekeeper had taken to hide her own belief in the supernatural from possible eavesdroppers. She might very evidently have spared her pains.

So Mrs. Mitters herself seemed to

think, as she went off to personally super-
intend the cutting, with especially particular care, of the thin bread and butter
for a poverty-stricken old woman, whose
sick fancy would certainly have been added
to the number of weary little unsatisfied
wants but for " Our Bobby."

CHAPTER IV.

ALLOWED TO BUY A PRIZE.

YOUNG man was lying one morning on a ledge of rock, looking down at one of Nature's pictures. To the left of his view, beneath him, was a little shore-built cottage, the sunlit blue-green sea was edging the land with a tiny line as of white swan's down, geraniums and nasturtiums blossomed brightly in the cottage windows, and a young girl sat in the cottage door, singing gaily, as accompaniment to the fingers which were moving so quickly in their work of bonnet making—one of those cottage bonnets that folks so greatly admired in those days, and seem somewhat inclined to laugh at, now that fashion has brought them into some slight use again.

Just as the young milliner had come to the end of the bonnet then in hand, another figure came upon the scene. A fisher lad came slouching up to the cottage door, with a furtive look at his hands as he did so. The singer heard the crunching of the pebbles, stopped her song, and looked up.

"How do you do, Stedman? Is it not a delightful morning?"

"Very, miss, and I'm very well, an' so's father an' mother an' all of us. But please, miss," sheepishly, "I've coomed along again to see, won't ye let me buy one o' them baskets o' yours for mother? She wants one real bad, she do, and I've worked well for the money."

The girl looked at him from top to toe with a merry smile, and shook her head.

"I'm ever so glad to hear that you have worked well, Jem, but I am afraid that I cannot let you have the basket yet."

" Oh, Miss Bobby ! " exclaimed the lad, looking more inclined to cry than to laugh. " You don't mean that, do you ?   You let every one help you but me ! "

The girl's lips quivered for a moment at that outburst; but there was still a little mischievous smile on her fair face as she said : " To help me, Jem ?   I thought you told me that you wanted the basket to please your mother ? "

" And so I do," was the eager answer. " I do want the basket for mother, and to please her, because you said that day as it was shame to me that she'd scarce never a smile on her face. But it don't hurt mother that I'd rather get the basket o' you than of any one else, so's to do ye a ha'porth o' help at the same time ; do it now ? "

" No, Jem, no," said the young waif more seriously. " And it is very good of you to think so kindly of me. But you know I take a pride in making my baskets nicely and prettily, and I never sell them to untidy folks."

Jem blushed, and glanced down at his great broad hands again. "Miss Bobby, you're too hard on a fellow, you are. I've reg'lar scrubbed at them, I have, for ten minutes afore I came to you, but the tar stains will show."

"Oh, yes, I was not thinking of your hands," said Miss Bobby. "They look quite fine to what they did last time you came. But look at your sleeves, and your hair, and your shoes."

Jem dropped his gaze from his hands to his feet, encased in gaping coverings. "The pedlar han't been round lately, and there bean't no more laces at home."

"A bit of string off one of your old nets would tie your shoes quite as neatly as bought laces," was the quiet answer; "and if you have not got a comb, you had better use some of your basket-money to buy one. Good-bye."

"Good-bye," muttered poor Jem Stedman in return, and he began to move away with a heart as heavy as his sea-going steps. But although Bobby had spoken with a firmness and decision, as though giving forth one of the laws of the Medes and Persians, she found it very difficult to be hard or stern. She looked after the fisherman, and began to relent.

" Stedman."

Somebody lying on a near ledge of rock, seeing and hearing all, himself unseen, had quite been prepared to hear that soft little call; but it came evidently unawares upon Jem. He raised his drooping head, and came back with a glad cry.

"Yes, miss," he asked eagerly; "have ye thought o' some way to forgive me?"

The bright head was shaken mischievously. "Ah, Jem! you must not ask too much, you know. But I think —I think—that perhaps—I will let you have the basket now, if you will promise, to please me, to try to be a tidier fellow in the future than you ever have been yet?"

She looked up with earnest simplicity at the tall, strong young man, at least two or three years older than herself, who stood before his gentle young mentor, and stammered out earnest promises that he would do his best to be a very pattern, in return for her present goodness to him. And then the watcher on the ledge lost sight of them both for a few minutes, as they entered the cottage to choose the desired basket.

Jem re-appeared at last with a dainty affair of white wicker with a crimson open-work border, which he was carrying as though it were at least as brittle and precious as eggshell china. His broad face was one beam of triumphant delight.

"An' ye'll use my money for yourself, Miss Bobby, now, won't ye?" he asked pleadingly.

"Yes, truly I will," was the frank answer. "It has just made up what I wanted for some new boots. I am going into the market town with my bonnets to-morrow morning, and I hope to bring my purchase back with me at night. I will pay your very actual shillings away for my boots in the shop, if all goes well.

But good-bye now. I cannot afford to play all the morning, if you can." And with another of those knowing little shakes of the head, she reseated herself at the cottage door, and resumed her work with a busy nimbleness of fingers that seemed determined to make up for their ten minutes' idleness.

Jem Stedman marched home past as many of his neighbours, and his neighbours' cottages, as he could well manage, and could scarcely keep his delighted chuckles from exploding in an exultant roar, as he heard one and another ejaculate,—

"My! If Jem Stedman ain't been let to buy one o' our Bobby's baskets!"

A little of his glory was crushed by one boy adding—"And he ain't none so tidy neither."

Jem was close to his own home then, and he made a plunge in at the door, feeling that he had done Bobby a wrong by carrying her basket above his untied shoes. He would have remedied the defect on the instant, had it been possible, but his mother and sister caught sight of the treasure lying so gingerly on the palms of his two outstretched hands, and sprang forward.

"Oh, Jem, how pretty!" they exclaimed together. "It's her very best pattern of all."

The fisher lad forgot his late discomfiture, and chuckled again as he replied: "Ay, 'tis pretty, isn't it; Miss Bobby said as I'd chose out the best. But take it, mother, it's for you, and my hands ache."

And then, shouting back: "It's our Bobby's to thank for it, not me," he ran out of the cottage again to escape from his mother's happy words of praise, and thankfulness for her boy's kindness.

"Oh, mother! what should us do without our Bobby?" sighed Lucy Stedman as she walked slowly round the table on which the well-made new market-basket had been placed. "Jem was getting to be a peck o' trouble afore she took to speakin' to him whiles."

" Ay, to be sure, an' so he was," was the grave answer; "but he's a rare good lad now, and our Bobby has a mother's blessin's, ye may be sure o' that, my girl."

Many a mother in Downfells, and around it, had cause to say the same.

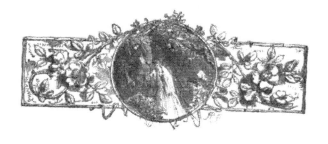

CHAPTER V.

A REGULAR LITTER ALL THROUGH.

" M I tidy enough to be allowed to buy a basket, please ? "

The ledge of rock was deserted now, and a young man, some years older than her last customer, stood before the Down-fells straw-worker. In face, in manner, in dress, in speech, this second would-be pur-chaser was as different to the last as is possible to imagine. Hands whiter than Miss Bobby's own; voice, if not so sweet, at least more highly cultivated; clothes, if suited to the easy negligence of country life, still of the latest cut, the best materials, and in the highest condition of orderliness.

Decidedly there was no trace of outward untidiness to be objected to this individual, as he stood there with a certain air of admiring deference, asking if he might be allowed to buy a basket.

There was a silence of some moments after he had asked his question. The blue eyes that had been raised with such kind, frank fearlessness to Jem Stedman were bent now still lower, and more fixedly, on another bonnet just begun to be fashioned of the woven straw. And the soft red lips, that had spoken for the sailor's benefit with a mixture of firmness and merry mischief, now remained closed. At last the new-comer spoke again, repeating his former question in a slightly altered form, and adding with a half laugh,—

"Pray be good enough to say that I am. I have even combed my hair within the past five minutes, to satisfy your requirements."

As he concluded that last word, the worker's fingers trembled so that she broke her needle, and the pink flush in her cheeks deepened to the deepest crimson as she forced herself to look up at length, and answer quietly,—

" The baskets I make are generally for poor people; they are not suitable for use up at the Hall, least of all suitable for you. Good morning. I have a patient in here."

" Oh ! wait, wait one moment," exclaimed the young man almost as eagerly as Jem Stedman had done, as the girl rose, and prepared to re-enter the cottage. " Do hear me one instant, please. That young fisherman I saw with you a few minutes since wanted the basket for his mother, and so do I for mine."

" Thank you," was the low, quiet reply. " I have none that I think would suit just now."

The colour in the gentleman's own cheeks deepened. " That—that—fellow —said that in—buying the basket he

wished—to—help you. I wish—to help
you too."

"I need no help, thank you," was yet
again the low, quiet reply; and the next
moment she was gone.

Harbston Deacon walked away, far away,
on and on along the sea-beach, until he
got out of sight of all other human beings
but himself, and of anything of a human
home; then he stood still, folded his arms,
gazed out over the sea, and muttered,—

"The fact is, she does not think me
tidy enough to have one of those baskets
of hers; that is the whole truth of the
matter, I'm convinced."

And Mr. Harbston Deacon was right.

As some compensation to the Downfells waif, for a secret consciousness that
he had not taken the care he might have
done to discover her identity, the old
curate-in-charge had very early in her
childhood undertaken her education; and
when she was ten years old she had made
her first use of what she had already
gained, by teaching the children of a bon-

net and basket-maker to read, in return for
instructions in the trade.

There was such eager competition for
the first little article of her manufacture in
Downfells and Summerton, that she had
said, by way of settlement of the matter,
that it should be for the person whom all
the neighbours should choose as the best
and nicest among them.

From that time forward, permission to
purchase one of Bobby's baskets had come
to be known as the invariable reward of
some fault rectified, or the testimony to
some virtue. So great had her gentle influence become that even the farmers' wives
would have a smile of satisfaction on their
faces, when they could tell a companion
that their new market-basket was, " one of
our Bobby's making."

So great had her influence become over
Harbston Deacon, during the past six
months, that his longing to possess one of
those baskets, with the maker's own free
consent, was greater than his artist longing had ever been to possess one of the
chef-d'œuvres of Italian art.   E

"But the fact is, she does not think me tidy enough to have one," he muttered as dolefully as Jem Stedman himself could have done. And he stood there gazing out over the still-seeming sea, and thought. Let his own life pass in review before him, from the earliest day he could remember up to the present time.

When he told himself, with so true a guess, that the golden-haired maiden of Downfells, the little worker in straw for daily bread, did not think him tidy enough to be allowed to become the purchaser of one of her baskets, he knew well enough that the tidiness in his case had nothing to do with his clothes, or his hair, or his hands. It was something in his life, in his deeds, in his character, that must, in her estimation, be wanting, or be out of order.

What could it be?

The rich, well-born, and influential Harbston Deacon felt that question to be about the most important one he had ever asked himself in his life. More than an hour he stood gazing out over the sea, and

then he flung himself down on the beach,
and lay there thinking for another two
hours longer. But with all his thinking,
it is a strange, true fact that his thoughts
gave him no clue.

The owner of Deepmoat Hall had ever
been a loving and obedient son, kind and
thoughtful; he was generous and true,
honest in heart and life, and upright.
Very few men could dare so closely to
look back through the bygone days; and
although Harbston was neither given to
vanity, nor self-satisfied, he knew it. And
yet—that gentle, blue-eyed girl would not
let him buy a basket.

The morning wore away, and the afternoon; evening was drawing on when the
young man presented himself again at the
cottage where "Bobby" had taken up her
abode for the time, because there was a
sick woman for its owner who needed
help.

The girl was again seated just outside
the door at her work, taking advantage of
the last of the daylight, when the lord of

the manor came near, and again her head
sank rather lower, and the soft rose of her
cheeks became crimson, as she heard the
sound of his firm, even steps approaching
her home. Her fingers began to tremble
as they had done in the morning, when he
spoke somewhat abruptly,—

" Miss Bobby ? "

A very tiny bow by way of acknow-
ledgment that she heard.

" I think with Jem Stedman, Miss
Bobby, that you are rather hard upon a
fellow. I do assure you that I would not
have been mean enough to ask for one of
those baskets, if I had felt that I had to
accuse myself of being wholly unworthy
to have one. I know and confess, as fully
as you do, that none of us are good or
righteous in the sight of God, but I do
dare to say that my heart and conscience
are well-nigh as clear as your own. I
have almost tried to-day, since you dismissed me so abruptly this morning, to
find some deed with which heartily to re-
proach myself, and it is a downright fact

that I cannot. You might let me have a basket!"

There was such a pleading tone in that concluding. exclamation that it evidently touched the little bonnet-maker's compassion. She showed some signs of relenting; the shining head was raised a little, and the red lips parted with a suspicion of a smile, which grew even broader as the clear voice said in a low, half-shy tone, "This is foolish. You know that my baskets can be no use to you."

"Ah! but indeed they can," was the eager answer. "As a sign of your approbation. You have raised and purified my tenants by teaching them to long for that, and I long for it too."

"But—but—I cannot give it," came the scarcely-breathed murmur; and the golden head sank down once more, even lower than before.

There was a pause; and there was a quiver in Harbston Deacon's own voice as he asked quietly at last, "Tell me— why not? What bad deeds do you believe—I declare, unjustly—are hidden in my past life?"

Again there was a pause. But the questioner was waiting for an answer, and evidently intended to wait for it, however long it might be in coming.

The girl put down her bonnet, and clasped her hands tightly, as though to gain courage and strength to speak. But with her best efforts the courage she contrived to seize was but a poor, faint little affair after all, to judge by the trembling, scarcely audible reply that came at last, not in her own words, but in those of two quotations :—

"'We have left undone those things that we ought to have done.' 'I know thy works, that thou art neither cold nor hot: I would thou wert cold or hot. So then because thou art lukewarm, and neither cold nor hot, I will spue thee out of my mouth.'"

There was silence before the young man asked, in tones almost as low as the girl's own, "You have wished for some time past to repeat these words to me, I·expect?"

"I have wished that you—might—think of them—yourself," came the truthful though so timid-voiced reply.

And then, silently, and with deep, burning colour in his face, Harbston Deacon turned and left her. His eyes were opened now. It was not the untidiness of what he had done, but the untidiness of what he had left undone, that forbade him to hope for the coveted basket, that forbade him to expect a place in the respect or esteem of the maker. Six months ago the owner of those fair estates had come home, full of high ideas of the duties the possession of such a property entailed upon him, full of grand resolves of what he would do for the comfort, the improvement, the welfare, of those about him.

Six months had gone by, and he had done —nothing. He had found things and people in a fair condition, he had seen nothing very loudly calling for improvement or remedy, he had found a most sweet and beautiful young girl elevating all about her with ennobling influence, and he had contented himself with watching her, with sauntering—harmlessly as he considered—through the days, and weeks, and months, looking on with a growing intensity of ad-·miration, and leaving a girl to do his work so far as her poverty and her weakness might enable her.

"So then because thou art lukewarm, and neither hot nor cold, I will spue thee out of my mouth."

The denunciation seemed burnt into his brain. When he heard them uttered by those soft, red lips, he had declared angrily in his heart that it was unfit, unmaidenly, that they should be thus uttered. In very truth, they were hard, ugly words, and they had stung deeply, and gone home.

"We have left undone those things that we ought to have done."

And he had dared to go and claim a basket with the plea that there was no untidiness about him ! His eyes were opened now, and he saw an untidiness far worse than that of poor, ignorant Jem Stedman's rough hair and untied shoes. There was an unused life lying behind him, littered through and through with a terrible, accusing, wasteful disorder of duties left undone.

*   *   *   *

Mr. Deacon had had enough, for that day, of the sea. He felt as though the innocent ocean had been telling him falsehoods, during all those morning hours whilst he had taken it into his communings as to whether he were not a model of moral tidiness. He climbed the cliffs now, and wandered into the fields, and flung himself down under the first thick, dark hedge he came to.

Meantime it was growing too dusk to see to thread needles, so Bobby put by her work, and leaving the sick cottager in the welcome companionship of a friend who had dropped in for a comfortable chat, she tied on her hat, and bounded up the steep path, to devote half an hour or so to her children friends in the village lying above.

Five minutes hence she was the centre of a circle in a grassy field, and gaily questioning her companions as to how they had been spending the past day.

" And what have you done, Bobby Moggins?" she asked at length of a broad-shouldered, rosy-cheeked young urchin, who had been hiding himself, as well as he

could, behind his companions during the questioning business. But it was no good. His turn came, and, digging a hole with his heel in the grass, he blurted out,—

"Ain't done nuffin, nuffin bad, nor nuffin. Slep' on the shore a bit o' the day, an' had my dinner, an' sat in the fields like now, an'—an'—that's all."

".Oh, Bobby!" sighed that gentle voice.
"Another day good for nothing, and gone!
Oh, Bobby! how dismal, how miserable!"
And there was such an echo of sadness in
those sweet tones that the unseen, unsuspected individual under the dark hedge
winced as though he had been struck, and
barely stifled a groan. As for the small
Laziness, Bobby Moggins, he began to cry,
putting his grubby brown fists into his
eyes, and muttering that he'd "go home
and get father's supper ready, 'stead o'
mother, if Miss Bobby ony wouldn't speak
no more like that."

And then the girl bent forward, and
kissed the grubby face, and said pityingly,—

"There, Bobby boy, I did not mean to
make you cry. It's not quite time to get
father's supper ready yet, so if you will
look up, and give me a nice bright smile,
like a good little fellow, I will tell you all
a little fairy tale that jumped into my head
to-day, while I was working at my bonnets."

Bobby Moggins was so much more given

to smiles than tears in a general way, that, what with the pardon and the promise, he found little difficulty in granting the condition; and then, all the children gathering up closer to their favourite, and with another unsuspected listener under the hedge, the young teacher began to add emphasis to a lesson already once before to-day given to a far older pupil than openmouthed young Bobby.

"I call my story," began "Our Bobby," "the story of

"The Cruel Little River.

" Once upon a time, beside a quiet, clean, pretty little village, and through bright, green fields, a beautiful river of clear, sweet, water murmured along, singing a sweet, happy song. Its song was not so loud as the songs of the birds who flew over it, and dipped their beaks into it, but it was very sweet and pleasant to all those who chose to listen. It ran along so swiftly and so merrily that the rosy-cheeked village children, with shouts and laughter,

would run races with it in the long summer evenings, when they played on its
banks, and gathered their hands full of
fresh, fragrant wild flowers.

"Sometimes, when the wind blew
freshly, the river would be as full of curves
and twists as a little boy's curls.   At other

times it would dimple all over, as though
it were smiling up at the bright blue sky.
And whatever it did, the people loved it,
for they said that it was a good little river.
It worked brightly and bravely; it was
never idle; it did its best to make the country, through which it flowed, cheerful and

healthy and happy. And the river itself
was very happy, and a lovely fairy lived in
the midst of its bright waters, called the
fairy 'Right Contentment.' "

" Can there be a fairy Wrong Contentment ? " murmured a little voice at this
point in the tale, very wonderingly.

The voice belonged to a certain little
maiden who early in this history sat sobbing under a tree, because secretly she
wished to have the best of her home's
" everything," and openly she declared her
belief that she got the worst. The story-
teller looked round at her for a moment
with an answering nod and smile—" You
shall hear, Nettie, whether there is, if you
keep your ears quite wide open a little
while longer."

" After the little river had gone on
brightly and merrily for some good time,
singing and laughing day by day over its
work, at length a change came—a very sad
and miserable one it was too—a house was
to be built in one of the bright green fields,
and men were set to dig away the earth for

its foundations; and as they dug it out, they threw it into carts, and drove off with it to the little river, and there cast it in to get it out of their way. They said,—

" ' The river runs so fast that the rubbish won't hurt it, for it will soon wash it away.'

"And the river laughed up at them— ' Oh, yes.' And the first few cartloads it did carry away with it, using it cleverly to fill in the holes in its bed.

"But the men poured in the cartloads more quickly, and the river came upon a heap it found rather hard to move. After trying a little while it said—' There! it does not hurt me; I shall let it alone.' And so it did, and tumbled itself over the mud instead of flowing easily along. In a few days the mud heap had grown so high, the river could no longer even tumble itself over it; but still it would not try to clear it away. It said,—

" ' Oh! never mind; I am not going to trouble myself. I am quiet here; the children can come, and dance and play beside me, I am contented.'

" And so it let itself be changed from a
bright sparkling, working stream into a
dull, stagnant pool, and the weeds grew
over it, and the waters lost their clearness,
and became dark and thick. And very
soon it was left all alone to its lazy sleep,
for mothers kept their little children away
from the bad, heavy air of the river that
had driven away Right Contentment, and
taken the pretty fairy's ugly, idle cousin
Wrong Contentment to live with it instead.

" The hot summer weather came, and the
stagnant river nearly dried away, and bad
sickly smells came from the muddy ditch
and half-dead weeds, and many of the people in the village became ill because of the
selfishly idle, cruel little river. Still, for
some time, Wrong Contentment had it all
her own way, and the people said,—

" ' Ah ! never mind ; we can't help it.'

" The idle river's bad example had done
that harm too, you see ; it taught the people
about it to think that there wasn't much
wrong in being idle. We cannot spend

useless days, ourselves, without teaching somebody else to waste the good time and strength that God has given us."

Bobby Moggins hung his head. He thought those words were very especially meant for him, and he remembered how his little sister Patty had said, an hour or so ago—"I don't see why I should go on with my sewin', Bob hasn't done nuffin all day."

But in reality a very different to Bobby Moggins was in the mind of the golden-haired lassie at that moment, and so some one lying hidden under the dark hedge guessed. Meantime the tale went on.

"The worthless little idle river said 'Never mind,' and the poor, foolish people said 'Never mind,' and so they suffered badly. But at last a brave, sensible man came to the place, and he said,—

"'Never mind, do you say? Can't help it, do you say? But I say that we can help it, and that we must. I, at least, am not contented with what is wrong. I am not contented to see every one about me sick

F

and miserable, when it is in our power to
be well and happy.'

" And he stirred up the right courage of
the people, and they set to work and drained
away the slothful, worse than good-for-nothing little river entirely, and there was an
end of it, and the fairy Wrong Contentment had to find another home."

" She won't come here, I hope," said one
of the elder children, laughing.

" Nay, indeed, I hope not," was the
cheerful reply; " and so, to keep her
away, we must not be content to stay here
any longer now, when other people are
waiting for us to help them to get supper
ready. Besides, you know that I have to
be up very early to-morrow for my long
walk to the town with my bonnets, so I
must get to bed early. Good-night everybody."

" Good-night, good-night," shouted
twenty voices in return; and then the
whole party sprang to their feet, and scam-
pered off together. And somebody who
had been lying under a dark hedge got

up with a very grave face, stretched his cramped limbs, and went home. He felt very wretchedly untidy just then.

"And they drained away the worse than good-for-nothing river," muttered Harbston Deacon to himself as he mounted the steps of Deepmoat Hall, "'and there was an end of it.' If there were an end of me, the next heir would step into my shoes; he could not do less for the good of the charge committed to him, he very well might do more."

CHAPTER VI.

SOME ONE ELSE AT THE COTTAGE ON THE BEACH.

HEN Mr. Deacon entered his own hall, he saw one of his men-servants, a native of the place, and called to him,—

"James, how far is it from here to the market-town?"

"A little over ten miles, sir," was the prompt reply, "to walk."

"*Over* ten miles!" was the aghast exclamation. "And how do the people from here get over there and back again?"

"Get over, sir?" repeated the man, looking a little puzzled.

"Yes, yes," rather impatiently.   "In what sort of carts, or things?"

"Oh, sir!" answered James, with a slight apologetic laugh.   "We don't have no carts for that bit of a journey.   Whiles the farmers may give a lift to an over-loaded lass, but mostly half a dozen or so steps out together, first dawning, and gets back home at nightfall, none so tired as you seem to think for."

"Umph," muttered his master, and then he turned into the drawing-room in search of his mother, and began rather abruptly,—

"Mother dear, don't you want some bonnets?"

"Want some bonnets!" exclaimed Mrs. Deacon.   "*Some* bonnets, my dear son; what can you mean?"

"Well, Mother," with a short laugh, and with his face flushing, "I suppose you cannot want *some* for your own immediate wear, but you might be glad of a few to give away.   The fact is, that I should be glad if you would buy all those

that the little ministering spirit of Downfells has by her just now, to save her
the twenty-mile walk to the town and
back, to sell them, that she means to take
to-morrow."

Mrs. Deacon raised her eyes from the
delicate little ivory casket she was carefully dusting. "Poor child!" she ejaculated pityingly, but at the same time
she looked rather keenly at her son. He
turned half aside, as he echoed,—

"Ay, poor child, indeed. I wish with
all my heart that you could find some
means to help her in a way that she would
accept, for I have heard something to-day
that makes me sorely afraid that, while
she is the helper of every one around her,
she herself suffers very many privations."

"She looks very happy, always."

"And so she would do, I believe, if
she were to have her head cut off, if only
she could know that by so suffering she
was saving some one else from losing a
finger."

"Yes," assented his mother quietly.

She herself thought very highly of the
little straw-worker, but she would rather
have preferred that the young owner of
Deepmoats should not speak of her quite
so zealously.

However, her quiet agreement did not
suffice for her son just that minute. At
another time he might have allowed it to
seem to do, and not have pressed his
wishes any more for the moment. But his
mind was full of the thought that it was
already late evening, and that Miss Bobby
would be setting out with the first streak
of the morrow's light on her long, long
tramp, over rough roads, in those worn-
out shoes he had seen on her little feet,
if nothing were done now to stop her.

These hard facts gave him courage to
repeat his request. And at length Mrs.
Deacon was fain to satisfy him by sending
off her maid to make a wholesale purchase
of straw bonnets; and then, and not till
then, did her son go off in reviving spirits
to sup by appointment with his neighbours
on the adjoining estate.

Mrs. Deacon had retired for the night when Harbston returned home; but he lost no time, when they met the next morning at the breakfast-table, in asking how she liked her new bonnets, and how many of them she had got.

"I have got none, I am sorry to say," answered his mother, in a genuine tone of regret. "Our Bobby offered to make me in the future any number I might wish to order, but she could not let me have those now finished. They were a commission from a buyer, who was to come into the market-town to-day on purpose to receive them. I am truly vexed, my son."

"Yes," said Harbston absently, and he turned, and gazed out over the sea as sadly as he had done yesterday.

"Is it a very bad road between here and the town, James?" he asked his young footman an hour later.

"Pretty baddish, some bits, sir," answered the man calmly. And his young master had some difficulty in stifling a sigh.

Mr. Deacon strolled down on to the beach the next day, and past the cottage where he had seen the bonnet-maker at work the day before yesterday. Instead of her graceful young figure clad in dark blue linsey, with the golden crown of hair on her head, and the golden straw slipping over her small fingers, a middle-aged woman sat in the doorway now, mending a fisherman's faded old jersey, and keeping up, meantime, a rough-voiced, shouting conversation with the invalid inside.

" Our Bobby were main sorry to leave her 'tendance on you, I can tell ye," shouted the needlewoman. " But when I saw how set upon staying to help the poor gipsy bodies she was, I couldn't do less nor offer to take her place wi' ye, specially now my man an' th' lads are away, and I ain't wanted at home."

There was a pause for a few moments, at least as far as the pedestrian listener was concerned. The invalid had asked a question apparently, in a less audible voice. Then came the answer.

" What was the matter with the gipsies,
do ye say? Deed then, that's more than
I know. All I can tell you is this.
When we'd got half-way back yesterday
evening, to Windy Common ye know,
there was a ragged, dark-faced child, maybe
twelve year old, sitting on the ground
a yard or two from a ragged tent, crying
as if her heart would break. Of course I
needn't tell ye as down went our Bobby's
bundles, and down went herself on her
knees, with her arms round the dirty brat
as if she'd never spoke up for cleanness
and tidiness in her life. It seems the
child's mother had been taken ill while
the party were on the tramp that day, and
so, while all the others had gone forward,
they'd just put up the tent, and left the
sick woman in it, and her girl, to take care
of themselves. And the sick woman had
got so much worse that the child was
fairly frightened out of her wits. Well,
the upshot of it was that Bobby went into
the tent to have a look at the gipsy, and
she came back in a minute with a white,

tearful face, begging one of us to see to you a bit, and to carry home her straw for her, and she'd be thankful to stay there a wee."

Another pause, and another question from inside, and again a reply—"Give us her money too, to bring home, do ye ask? Nay then, neighbour, for sure ye know our Bobby better nor that! We did ask her wouldn't she let us bring it for her for safety. But she said, so quiet and simple like as shut our mouths I can't say how: 'Why so? You see I may most likely want it for these poor things.' And so she kept it, and her tea and sugar, and new boots; an' I'll be bound all 'ull go to those beggars before she gets back, and she'll just go next to barefoot again all through the bitter winter."

A sound that was something between a groan and a sob came as a wind-up to this declaration, but it was uttered by one who was too far off for the loud-voiced woman to hear it. And then Harbston Deacon wandered on again along the sea-

shore, till he reached the point where he
had halted that other day.   His heart had
been heavy then, with the conviction that
he had somehow earned the disapproba-
tion of a young and desolate girl.   It was
heavier now with the dread that some
harm might come to her; and during the
past few weeks he had been learning, with
ever-growing force day by day, to think
that a world without that sweet face in it,
and that golden head, would be a world
as murky of hue as the sea he was now
gazing at.

CHAPTER VII.

WINDY COMMON.

WILD, dreary region, well named Windy Common. It was the middle of the October of a particularly fine and beautiful year, but on that dismal tract the chill, damp blasts of winter seemed already to have taken up their abode. Many commons are very beautiful, but such was decidedly not this horrible Windy Common, excepting in so far as the grimness of utter, bare, far-stretching desolation has, of itself, a strange, unfathomable beauty of its own, for one's imagination in some rare moods. However one of these rare moods was not Harbston Deacon's, as he stood on the edge of it about one o'clock, the day after he had heard the news of "Our Bobby's" having chosen it for her latest place of temporary residence.

The owner of Deepmoat Hall, and its beautifully luxuriant surroundings, stood and shivered as he gazed at this portion of his property. He had never even seen this short cut between Downfells village and the market-town before. When he had gone to the town, on business or pleasure, he had always driven; and a walk of ten miles, five out and five in, to see a place that he had been told by his agent was particularly unremunerative and ugly, was not at all to his taste. He had come now not to see the Common, but to see one whom he also had learnt to think of in his heart as "Our Bobby."

He had a sort of jealous feeling that she had no personal right whatever to devote herself to vagabond gipsies, that she was a part of the property belonging to the estate as much as one of the roses in the Deepmoats garden, and infinitely more precious, and to be retained more resolutely. He had come now to demand her return.

At ten o'clock that morning he had found Jem Stedman sitting on the edge of a boat on the beach, indulging in a downright hearty cry, and as careless of who might see him in that baby state as a baby itself might be. Early as it was he had already been over to Windy Common to take a new home-made loaf from his mother to Miss Bobby, and to see how it fared with her. And it fared so badly, according to his way of thinking, that there was some excuse for his exhibition of affectionate grief.

"We ain't none of us to go near her, sir, she says, not no more, till she lets us know," he stuttered amidst his sobs. "And—and—I can't do wi'out seein' her, nor none of us can't."

"Of course we cannot," was the decided answer. "But what is her reason for forbidding us to go near her—do you know?"

"Oh, yes! I knows fast enough," was the dreary reply, and Jem's tears ceased to flow, as though his thoughts of sorrow had grown too great to admit any longer of even that relief. "I knows well enough. It's all of a piece with the rest of her. The gipsy woman turns out to ha' got a bad sort o' fever, and 'Our Bobby' is to stop in the middle of it herself, but o' course never a one else is to do a hand's turn o' help for her, for fear we'd run any risk too. As if I wouldn't a sight sooner die o' th' fever myself than have to live here if she does! But she says if ever a one of us goes anigh the tent again, she'll just beg all the baskets back, and take herself right away into the world away from us all. She wouldn't even let me come within a score o' yards of her."

"But she shall let me," muttered Harbston Deacon, with his handsome face set and white as none had ever seen it before, as he strode rapidly back to the

Hall, and, summoning Mrs. Mitters, desired her to put up in a basket anything
and everything in the way of soups and
jellies and fruits that the house contained.

The dainties were soon packed, and
James brought them to his master, with
the request to know where he was to carry
the weighty basket.

" Nowhere," was the answer; and Mr.
Deacon took it in his own arms, and
walked off with it—"Looking so as you
couldn't dare so much as to say to him,
Very well, sir," said James on returning
to the housekeeper, whose private soliloquy
on the affair afterwards was a murmured—

" Well, well, it needs no second sight
to see where that basket's gone. And it's
not I that see any trouble in that either,
for fairy or water-sprite she may be, but a
little lady she is, and a blind bat could see
that with half an eye. And may be she
would be the one to put, a little of the
energy into him as is the one thing as the
dear young master lacks."

Her master looked little like lacking

G

energy, however, as he kept up the rapid pace with which he set out for the whole of the five miles between his home and the Common, and with the heavy supply of invalid comforts in his arms. On the edge of Windy Common he paused a moment to shudder at its dismalness, and to take a look round for the gipsies' tent. He discovered it at last, still at some distance, and again set off to reach it. But that he was destined not to do at all, for when he was within thirty yards or so of it the self-constituted young nurse came outside, caught sight of him, and raising her hands suddenly to her head as though in pain, she flew from the tent as if she supposed it was on fire. When Jem Stedman had made his appearance early in the morning she had done the same—an unconscious imitation of the bird that flutters before one on the lower twigs of the hedge, to lure danger away from its nest. But it was for the sake of the visitors, and not for the occupants of the tent, that the young girl adopted the bird's artifice.

Mr. Deacon changed his course from the tent, and came towards the bonnet-maker, who stopped in her flight at last, and, facing him, waved him back, exclaiming in a tone of grave authority, such as astonished him into obedience,—

"Do not come any nearer. I hoped that you, as well as the villagers, would hear from Jem Stedman that I do not wish any one to come about here for the present. The fever is a terribly infectious one."

" I have heard from Jem Stedman, and that is why I have come," was the half-dogged answer.

The hearer clasped her hands in distress. " Oh, how can you !" she cried impulsively. " You are content to do nothing for your people, you at least might shun being the means of sowing suffering and sorrow amongst them ! "

" Don't fear," was the angry-sounding answer. " I will not go near any of your lambs. I will keep away from the villages around, and from my home too if you like. But if I choose to risk my own life by coming to this tent every day, I suppose I have as much right to do it as you."

The girl's face paled, and tears sprang into the blue eyes. " No, no," she said, with quivering lips, and, in her new agitation, herself forgetful of the distance she had meant to maintain between them. " I am risking my life because this poor creature must have some one to nurse her, but it would be wicked of you to do it for no good."

" It is some good," he replied gently, " at least I hope so, to show you that you have a friend's sympathy in your dangerous labour of love."

The next moment he added with a bitter laugh—"And there is even a greater good too, and that according to your own showing, in putting my worthless life in jeopardy. 'And they drained away the worse than good-for-nothing river, and there was an end of it.' I was under the hedge when you told the children that, and I know you meant it for me."

" Oh ! " with a quick looking-up and

shy fear, "indeed, indeed I did not know that you were near."

"No, I am quite aware of that; but you cannot deny that you were thinking of me?"

There was no answer, no word, only a deepening and a deepening of the burning flush in the girl's cheeks; and somehow, as Harbston Deacon gazed at her, the bitterness and the hardness faded from his face, the space between the two grew still less, and he said in low tones,—

"You may go on telling as many fairy tales against me as you please, if only you will go on thinking of me."

And then he put out his hand to take hers; but that action brought her to her every-day senses again, and with a little cry of dismay she sprang away backwards, away from him once more.

"Oh! do go, please go," she pleaded with downcast eyes, and the rosy colour fading away to whiteness. "And you will not come any more, will you?"

"I cannot promise quite all that," said the young man boldly.

Of course he would have resented the imputation from any one that he shared the belief, regarding Miss Bobby, of Mrs. Mitters, his housekeeper; still it is the fact that at that minute, for the first time since he first saw her standing at the side-door of Deepmoat Hall, begging thin bread and butter for a poor old woman, he fully realized that she was no fairy or fleeting water-sprite, but a genuine human being, capable of having her own little private hopes and fears and prepossessions, as well as any other gentle human girl. The discovery rather interfered with her present authority over him. And she grew the more timid as he grew braver.

"Oh! please, pray, say that you will not come," she murmured entreatingly. "It hurts me to have you—any one come here into danger needlessly."

"Then I will not come into danger," he retorted, "unless you compel me to. If you will promise to come outside the tent every day at ten o'clock, and to eat every day a good share of the things that I shall bring for you and your patient, then I will promise only to come just near enough to see that you are safe. If not, or if you break your word, I will come one night,— that is the most dangerous time for catching illnesses, is it not?—and keep watch with my head against the canvas of the tent yonder, until the morning."

Bobby shuddered, and turned paler than ever at the threat as she gave her promise. She little guessed the news those white cheeks told to her companion, nor how, all unconscious as she was, she sent him away with his heart thrilling with a happiness so great that for the time it blinded him even to her peril. He felt inclined to bless the fever which had betrayed her into showing her anxious longing for his safety.

CHAPTER VIII.

MRS. MITTERS HAS IMAGINATION.

"Not every one that saith unto Me, Lord, Lord, shall enter nto the kingdom of heaven ; but he that doeth the will of My Father which is in heaven."

ATURDAY had come, and this text was the heading of a sermon that the parson of Downfells with Somerton intended to preach the next day. It was written on paper yellow with age, for he had unearthed it from a pile which he had written and preached nearly forty years ago. It had been full of Christian fervour and energy then, and may be it might touch some conscience now, although his own heart had long since forgotten its teaching—so long that he had greater faith in the spirit of that faded writing than in anything that his present powers could produce.

But while the sermon lay out on the writing table, the scholar himself sat beside a cheerful wood fire blazing merrily away on his hearth. It was November now, and both the warmth and brightness of a fire were necessary antidotes to outside dreariness. He had drawn close up to it in the hope that it might be some antidote to his own. He had a Greek tragedy in his hand, but the book was upside down. The critical question over which he had been puzzling for the past week, as to the correct translation of a particular line, appeared to be a matter now of utter insignificance even to the critic.

Within the present half-hour his old servant had burst into his library, crying bitterly, and exclaiming—

"Oh! sir, our Bobby's down with the fever now herself. The doctor from the town has come over to tell us, and to beg us, from herself, not to go anigh her. She's bad as bad, he says. And oh! sir, if she's took, what ever will become of us? There's ne'er a one else, sure, hereabouts, to keep us up."

And the grieving woman was right. She took herself off back to her kitchen, leaving her master staring at the text of his own sermon—

"Not every one that saith unto Me, Lord, Lord, shall enter into the kingdom of heaven; but he that doeth the will of My Father which is in heaven."

He was heard to say, "Lord, Lord," very often, every Sabbath-day, and many other times in the course of his routine duty. The young ministering spirit of Downfells had been heard to say it very little, but her life had spoken with the pure sound of refined silver—

"I do the will of my Father which is in heaven."

And at last the Greek tragedy dropped from the scholar's hand, and the old man sank down on his knees, bowing his grey head upon his chair as he moaned—

"Oh! my Father, cut short, if Thou wilt, the thread of my useless life; but spare this young life. Oh! in Thy mercy, for the furtherance of Thine own kingdom upon earth, let it be Thy good will to spare it."

Immediately after his quickly-eaten twelve-o'clock dinner the old clergyman swallowed a few drops of camphor, hung a bag of camphor round his neck, bathed his face and hands in camphor water, and went out.

Three hours later, as he was returning home along the beach, he saw Mr. Harbston Deacon coming slowly towards him, with bent head and set white face. He called to him.

"Mr. Deacon, I have a message to you from our Bobby."

The young man raised his head with a sudden start. "To me!" he exclaimed,

and sprang forward. But the clergyman
stopped him.

"Stay where you are," he cried, with a
new accent of dignity and resolution in
his voice. "I have only been with our
dear and precious invalid five minutes,
and since then I have let these strong sea
breezes do all they can to blow the hut's
atmosphere from me; but I am determined to run the least possible risk I can
of spreading illness amongst our people.
Their nurse and comforter and helper is
laid low, so that it is more than ever in-
cumbent upon you and me to keep trouble
away from those committed to our charge.
If you will just sit down where you are,
I will sit down here, and speak to you
against the wind as well as I am able."

Harbston Deacon flung himself down
with an air of impatient misery. "But
the message," he said, "the message?"

"Yes, yes, the message," answered Mr.
Robinson, with a sudden look of fresh intelligence in his eyes. "By the bye," he
added, in a tone of more earnest friendli-

ness, " there were several messages, I
believe, or pieces of information very
much of that nature. She told me that
she was quite sure that a great deal of the
suffering of her illness was spared her, by
being in the hut you have had built up for
them out there on the Common, and that
the grapes and jelly had been the greatest
comfort to her the past two days. As for
nursing, the gipsy woman's child seems
to have learnt wonders in that way from
our Bobby, and the poor woman herself is
making the most of her returning strength
to take care of her nurse."

The utterness of despair that had been
apparent on Harbston's countenance disappeared as he listened. He, also, had
been told with the greatest possible amount
of emphasis by the gipsy girl, who had
come out to speak to him that morning
instead of Bobby, that the fresh victim of
the fever was "as bad as bad," and he
had given up all hope of ever seeing her
again, on the instant. But the quiet way
in which Mr. Robinson was giving his

information about her little speeches seemed to put matters in a less desperate light, and his tone was a shade more reasonable as he asked again,—

"But what was the message that you began by telling me she sent? Is it anything she wants taken to her?"

"It is something she wants, yes," answered the old clergyman, gravely. "But not taken to her. It is not for herself. She is growing troubled about the people here, and the children. She is afraid that the little ones will forget all she has taught them, and she wants you and me to set up schools for them. I have promised to do my best, and she says she believes that you will give the money for the building. Then she wants something done in the way of blankets and coals for the poor folks this winter. I thought, for my part, that they'd always managed well enough for themselves hitherto; but she declared, with tears, that one of the old men who died last January, died literally of the bitter cold he suffered.

"And another thing she seems very anxious about—she says she has often thought of it—if you would get some of the men and lads, once or twice a week, up to look at some of the treasures or curiosities you have brought from abroad; she says she is sure it would do much towards keeping them from the public-house. And I dare say it might.

"But good afternoon now, I must be going, for I have promised to get a word with Charles Granby too, if I can, before I return home to tea. Our Bobby says that this is the evening on which he and his wife are always most inclined to quarrel. He finds a good deal of untidy Saturday cleaning, I suppose, and then goes off in bad humour to waste his week's wages at the public-house. I am going to offer him an hour's overtime work, mending an old table at the Parsonage, and then he will get his tea with Betty in the kitchen; and by the time he goes home, no doubt his wife will be ready and glad to welcome him. Good-bye."

"Good-bye," returned Harbston Deacon; and then, while the clergyman mounted to the village to make an unusual attempt on a week-day to keep one of his flock in the right path, Harbston walked on to a cutting in the cliffs nearer to Deepmoat Hall.   Once in his walk he stopped, and turning to the wintry-grey sea muttered,—

"She thinks that she will die, and so she gives us her teaching for the last time, that we may learn to follow her to heaven."

And Harbston Deacon was right. Golden-haired Bobby felt her head heavy with its agony of pain, and her fair, sweet face burning with the fire of disease, and she fully believed that the dimmed blue eyes were about to close on earth for heaven.   Many another shared her thought.

Mrs. Mitters sat in her own apartment dropping quiet tears into her tea, as already in imagination she saw a little pure white marble gravestone in the village churchyard, bearing the simple but all-sufficient inscription in gold letters,—

"OUR BOBBY."

Many long years would pass before the love would die out, or be forgotten, that would be conjured up by the sight or sound of those two words.

Mrs. Mitters sat crying over her tea in her own little room, and her master and mistress sat sad and sorrowful at their tea in the great drawing-room.

"Mother," muttered the young man, in a voice that told of a half-breaking heart—"mother, she would have been a daughter that the noblest mother might have joyed to have."

And Mrs. Deacon rose, and, coming to her son, drew his head into her arms as though he were still a child, as she answered tenderly, "My boy, my only one, I know it. But of what good such a confession now? Live, my son, to prove that you could have been worthy of her."

H

CHAPTER IX.

AND "OUR BOBBY" TO THE END.

NE lovely warm May evening, Mrs. Mitters had betaken herself to the field in which, a year ago, she had sat on one side of the great oak-tree, while a fairy tale was told on the other. But just as she entered the field she beat a hasty, unobserved retreat again, and took a short, thoughtful stroll in another direction, with a very contented smile on her pleasant, honest face.

At the moment Mrs. Mitters looked towards the oak tree, two people met beneath its shade, and Scotch eyes are very good for distances. The worthy housekeeper had no wish to intrude her company upon the companions under the oak tree.

When it is said that two people met beneath the tree, it may be as well to mention that a girl had been sitting under it for some little time, reading, and was a good deal startled when some one came quickly up to her, and said with a tone of eager gladness,—

"Good evening, Miss Bobby. I have caught you at last!"

"Oh, Mr. Deacon, you said this afternoon that you were going this evening over to the town."

"And so I have been," was the mischievous, laughing answer. "Galloped there and back again. I don't know what poor Meteor will think of you for causing me to ride her so hard!"

"I—I don't know what you mean," came the stammering reply.

"Nay, nay," came the lower but still

smiling answer. "That is not quite so truthful as you generally are. You know perfectly well that you have condemned me to this subterfuge, to get at you without a guardian hedge of children or old women about you. Why are you afraid of me since you have come back to Downfells, our Bobby—*my* Bobby?"

"I—I——" began a quivering pair of red lips. She wanted to declare that she was not afraid of him, but the words would not come.

Harbston Deacon did not press for an answer. He asked another question instead.

"Bobby, *my* Bobby." He felt that it was rather daring of him a second time to drop the "Miss," and a second time to utter that "my"; but after all he could run faster than she could, if she tried to escape, and then again, he spoke the "my" in such a very low tone that she could pretend not to hear it, if she liked. And so he repeated it a third time, as if he liked it.

" Bobby, *my* Bobby, may I buy a basket now ? "

" Yes, if you wish," came the timid reply; and with a colour in the delicate cheeks almost as deep as when they were dyed with the fever she added, " I—I have made one—for you, if you will have it."

" Thank you," said Harbston.   His own lips were quivering now.   He came a step nearer.   " And since you think me worthy of the basket then, you will give me that other thing I wish for, will you not ? "

" I—I don't know what it is."

" Don't you ? " with an attempt to smile, but with something much more like a sob of emotion.   " The thing I long for now is the little hand that made it, that with this hand clasped in mine I may have strength to walk through life as our Bobby would have me.   May I not then take it, and keep it ? "

" Your   mother———"   muttered   the trembling lips.

" Nay, that plea against my good, and

the good of my tenants, will avail you nothing. I have my mother's blessing on my love."

The girl looked up quickly, with the light of love and hope shining in her eyes. "But I am no one," she exclaimed doubtfully—"I mean, I have no name, no family. None know who I am, nor whence I came, and you are of an ancient and grand race."

"Nothing like so ancient nor so grand as yours," was the laughing answer, as he took the soft fingers, and, drawing them through his arm, began to move towards his home. "When I first came here, more than twelve months ago, I was told that you were either a fairy or one of Neptune's daughters. I have heard the same thing many a time since."

For a few moments there was silence, then those red lips murmured again pathetically, "Oh! let me go, please. Some day, else, you may learn to be sorry."

"Never," ejaculated Harbston Deacon, with an earnestness that made his voice sound almost stern. The next instant, however, he stood still, and, clasping both her hands in his own, he said gently,—

"Forgive me for letting you trouble yourself with even these fears for a moment. They are phantom fears, and would have been so under any circumstances, but they are especially so now, since I, my mother, and Mr. Robinson, all know who you are—your name, your position in life, the place your father held before his death as a rising member of the English bar. You have one aunt, the only relation, she believes, that you have still surviving. Whilst you were ill Mr. Robinson hunted up a clue as to your identity he had found long ago, and then, amidst other occupations, dropped again. Now he has followed it out, and we have only been waiting until you were quite strong again to tell you. But whether you are Mildred Merton or anything else to the world, you are still to me my Bobby."

And when she sat, three years later, on

the beach with a "Mumma's Bobby" of
her own in her happy arms, the villagers
still smiled their love and sympathetic joy
at—

"OUR BOBBY."

Butler & Tanner, The Selwood Printing Works, Frome, and London.

THE POPULAR SERIES OF

NINEPENNY BOOKS FOR THE YOUNG.

WELL ILLUSTRATED.

"BUY AN ORANGE, SIR?" or, A History of Jamie Woodford.

DARE TO BE SINGULAR; or, The Story of Ned Barlow the Miner.

THE SURPRISE; or, Little Robert and his Dog.

DON'T SAY SO; or, You may be Mistaken.

OUR VILLAGE GIRLS. By HETTY BOWMAN.

JOHN PHILIPS; or, Happy Homes for Working Men.

RUTH ALLEN; or, The Two Homes.

IDA BOYTON'S VILLAGE LIFE.

JACK, THE SAILOR BOY. Twenty Illustrations.

THE TRAVELLER. Twenty Illustrations.

THE LOST TRUNK. Illustrated.

DUTY IS SAFETY; or, Troublesome Tom. Twenty Illustrations.

THE HERON'S PLUME. Illustrated.

THE WHITE PIGEON. Illustrated.

GRANDMAMMA PARKER; or, The Father's Return. Twenty-four Illustrations.

FRANK BEAUCHAMP; or, The Sailor's Family. Twenty Illustrations.

MARTIN CROOK, and the ROSE AND NIGHT-INGALE. Illustrated.

THE FALL OF PRIDE. Illustrated.

LONDON : THE BOOK SOCIETY, 28, PATERNOSTER ROW, E.C.
Order through your local Bookseller ; or a copy will be sent from the Society (post free) on receipt of published price.

6

NEW BOOKS

JUST PUBLISHED BY

THE BOOK SOCIETY.

PAGE, SQUIRE, AND KNIGHT..
A Romance of the Days of Chivalry. By W. H. DAVENPORT ADAMS, Author of "Success in Life," "Boys and their Ways," "Great Shipwrecks," &c. With 113 Illustrations, 17 Full-page. Price 5s.

STONES CRYING OUT.
Rock Witnesses to the Narratives of the Bible, collected from Palestine, Arabia, Assyria, Nineveh, and Egypt. By L. N. R., Author of "The Book and its Story," and "The Missing Link." Handsomely bound, with over 100 Illustrations. Price 3s. 6d.

THE BOOK AND ITS STORY; or, The History of the Bible in all Ages.
A Narrative for the Young. By L. N. R. Twenty-seventh Edition. 500 pages. Illustrated. Price 3s. 6d.

STORIES OF CHILD LIFE IN PROSE.
Edited by JOHN GREENLEAF WHITTIER. 300 pages, Crown 8vo. 90 Illustrations. Cloth elegant, 3s. 6d.

MEN OF MARK. Short Biographies of Celebrated Men. By MISS BRIGHTWELL. Cloth extra, gilt edges, 3s. 6d.

JANET CAMERON; or, The Lighthouse.
A Tale of Scottish Life. Well Illustrated, handsomely bound, gilt edges, 3s. 6d.

LIP SINS; or, Cannibal Propensities.
By the Author of "God's Tenth," etc., etc. Crown 8vo. Price 2s. 6d.

PRECIOUS TRUTHS FOR EVERY ONE.
By S. M. HAUGHTON. In very large type, suitable for the aged. Illustrated, 320 pages. Price 3s. 6d.

TRY, AND TRY AGAIN.
Being an Outline of the Lives of Two Youths who became Clergymen of the Church of England. By OLD JONATHAN (Rev. Dr. Doudney). Price 3s. 6d.

FROM OUT THE DEEP.
A Story of Cornish Life. By an Old Cornish Boy. Illustrated, handsomely bound, gilt edges. Price 3s. 6d.

LONDON: THE BOOK SOCIETY, 28, PATERNOSTER ROW, E.C.
Order through your local Bookseller; or a copy will be sent from the Society (post free) on receipt of published price.
7

CPSIA information can be obtained
at www.ICGtesting.com
Printed in the USA
BVOW08s2023260417
482407BV00011B/178/P